D0105893

THE BEDFORD SERIES IN HISTORY AND CULTURE

The Great Awakening

A Brief History with Documents

Related Titles in
THE BEDFORD SERIES IN HISTORY AND CULTURE
Advisory Editors: Lynn Hunt, University of California, Los Angeles
David W. Blight, Yale University
Bonnie G. Smith, Rutgers University
Natalie Zemon Davis, Princeton University
Ernest R. May, Harvard University

THE BEDFORD SERIES IN HISTORY AND CULTURE

The Great Awakening
A Brief History with Documents

Thomas S. Kidd
Baylor University

BEDFORD/ST. MARTIN'S   Boston   ◆   New York

For Bedford/St. Martin's

Executive Editor for History: Mary V. Dougherty
Director of Development for History: Jane Knetzger
Developmental Editor: Dale Anderson
Editorial Assistant: Laurel Damashek
Senior Production Supervisor: Joe Ford
Production Associate: Sarah Ulicny
Executive Marketing Manager: Jenna Bookin Barry
Project Management: Books By Design, Inc.
Text Design: Claire Seng Niemoeller
Indexer: Books By Design, Inc.
Cover Design: Liz Tardiff
Cover Art: George Whitefield Preaching by John Collet (c. 1725–1780). Bridgeman Art Library.
Composition: Stratford/TexTech
Printing and Binding: RR Donnelley & Sons Company

President: Joan E. Feinberg
Editorial Director: Denise B. Wydra
Director of Marketing: Karen Melton Soeltz
Director of Editing, Design, and Production: Marcia Cohen
Manager, Publishing Services: Emily Berleth

Library of Congress Control Number: 2007925326

Manufactured in the United States of America.

2   1   0
f   e   d   c

For information, write: Bedford / St. Martin's, 75 Arlington Street, Boston, MA 02116 (617-399-4000)

ISBN-10: 0-312-45225-X
ISBN-13: 978-0-312-45225-4

Acknowledgments

Acknowledgments and copyrights are continued at the back of the book on page 151, which constitutes an extension of the copyright page.

Foreword

The Bedford Series in History and Culture is designed so that readers can study the past as historians do.

The historian's first task is finding the evidence. Documents, letters, memoirs, interviews, pictures, movies, novels, or poems can provide facts and clues. Then the historian questions and compares the sources. There is more to do than in a courtroom, for hearsay evidence is welcome, and the historian is usually looking for answers beyond act and motive. Different views of an event may be as important as a single verdict. How a story is told may yield as much information as what it says.

Along the way the historian seeks help from other historians and perhaps from specialists in other disciplines. Finally, it is time to write, to decide on an interpretation and how to arrange the evidence for readers.

Each book in this series contains an important historical document or group of documents, each document a witness from the past and open to interpretation in different ways. The documents are combined with some element of historical narrative—an introduction or a biographical essay, for example—that provides students with an analysis of the primary source material and important background information about the world in which it was produced.

Each book in the series focuses on a specific topic within a specific historical period. Each provides a basis for lively thought and discussion about several aspects of the topic and the historian's role. Each is short enough (and inexpensive enough) to be a reasonable one-week assignment in a college course. Whether as classroom or personal reading, each book in the series provides firsthand experience of the challenge—and fun—of discovering, recreating, and interpreting the past.

Lynn Hunt
David W. Blight
Bonnie G. Smith
Natalie Zemon Davis
Ernest R. May

Preface

The Great Awakening: A Brief History with Documents examines the most significant religious and cultural upheaval in the history of colonial America: the First Great Awakening. This series of revivals, concentrated in the northern colonies from 1740 to 1743, dramatically changed and challenged the colonial churches. By the 1760s, it had spread to the South, setting the stage for the incredible growth of evangelical Christianity across the United States in the early Republic. The Great Awakening gave birth to American evangelical Christianity, which came to dominate much of American culture through the Civil War and continues to exercise influence in American politics today. From the outset, the Great Awakening was no polite, pious affair, but a deeply controversial spiritual movement that, to some observers, contained dangerous social implications. Some later scholars have even argued that the Great Awakening helped prepare the colonists for the American Revolution. The documents here illuminate the drama of spiritual conversions, noisy evangelical meetings, and the cultural arguments that the Great Awakening generated.

The book's introduction gives an overview of the Great Awakening, details the emergence of contending factions, and assesses the Great Awakening's consequences for American colonial history and the American Revolution. Although historians have conventionally described the debates over the Great Awakening as a contest between "New Lights" (supporters of the revivals) and "Old Lights" (opponents of the revivals), this book shows that it actually produced three main camps: moderate evangelicals, antirevivalists, and radical evangelicals. Moderate evangelicals supported the revivals but wanted to control their extremes; they correspond to the traditional "New Lights." Antirevivalists, or "Old Lights," thought the revivals had little to no godly merit and were, in fact, socially dangerous. The third group, the radicals, actively promoted and took part in the revivals, seeing in them great new possibilities for spiritual power. This group endorsed an individualistic theology of the Holy Spirit. This belief led many untutored laypeople—ordinary white men, women, children; African Americans; and Native Americans—to become, at times, exhorters, preachers, visionaries, and prophets. Although much historical attention has been given to the moderate evangelicals and antirevivalists, recent historians have begun to excavate the radicals as well. This history with documents aims to include the voices of the radicals as well as those of other camps.

The documents in this volume demonstrate the many tensions created by the revivals. They represent well-known figures of the Great Awakening, including Jonathan Edwards and George Whitefield, as well as personalities almost totally unknown until now, such as radical revivalist Daniel Rogers and Connecticut's Mercy Wheeler, who claimed to be miraculously healed in a 1743 meeting. Most of the documents focus on events and arguments rather than formal theology. They range from pastors' sermons to the spiritual experiences of slaves, Native Americans, and farm women and men. They are organized chronologically within each topic to give a feel for the key developments and disagreements in the Great Awakening.

The first group of documents focuses on Jonathan Edwards's 1735 Northampton, Massachusetts, awakening. The itinerant ministry of the most famous revivalist, George Whitefield, is examined in the second set of documents. The third set gives representative accounts of major revivals and a wonderful assortment of conversion narratives and spirit-filled experiences, from Mohegan minister Samson Occom's conversion to Mercy Wheeler's healing. The fourth set illustrates attempts to define the boundaries of the evangelical movement, from public debates over the legitimacy of the revivals to the arrest and humiliation of the radical revivalist James Davenport. In the fifth group, the accounts move to the colonial South, where evangelicals had to confront the issue of slavery more directly than in the North. Finally, the last document set explains the origins of the separatists and Baptists in New England and their fight for religious liberty across the colonies. Not only do the documents collected in this volume exemplify the broad range of religious practices and debates in the Great Awakening, but many of them have been successfully tested with students in my own undergraduate courses.

This book contains a number of pedagogical aids to help readers. Each document is introduced with a headnote identifying the author, context, and purpose of the document. Footnotes help explain obscure references in the documents. The chronology following the documents will help readers contextualize the major events of the Great Awakening. A list of questions for consideration will help stimulate class discussions or writing assignments. The extensive bibliography will help any professor or student wishing to know more about the subjects addressed here, and the index will serve as a guide to find specific people, events, and themes. On the whole, the book is designed to introduce the Great Awakening in an accessible but challenging framework, so that students will appreciate the significance of this seminal religious event in America's history.

A NOTE ABOUT THE TEXT

Many of the documents feature irregular spelling and punctuation, which was common in the eighteenth century. For particularly irregular usages, I have modernized spelling and punctuation. Words spelled out that were originally abbreviated or omitted are indicated by letters in brackets. Because most of the selections are excerpted from larger documents, I have indicated omissions of text by ellipses.

ACKNOWLEDGMENTS

I have had a great deal of assistance in preparing this book. Thanks to my research assistant, Jonathan Reid, who originally prepared most of the documents for the manuscript. My spring 2005 Baylor University course on the First and Second Great Awakenings inspired me and helped form much of the content here. Thanks also to the kind editorial assistance of Mary Dougherty, Jane Knetzger, Shannon Hunt, Laurel Damashek, Emily Berleth, and others at Bedford/St. Martin's. I deeply appreciate the time taken by John Fea, Messiah College; Timothy Hall, Central Michigan University; Janet Lindman, Rowan University; Rodger Payne, Louisiana State University; Sarah Purcell, Grinnell College; and Erik Seeman, University at Buffalo, SUNY, to read and comment extensively on the manuscript. Thanks also to my developmental editor, Dale Anderson, for his remarkably helpful efforts toward improving the book's final form. Thanks, as always, go to my wonderful wife, Ruby, and my children, Jonathan and Joshua Kidd. This book is dedicated to my parents, Michael and Nancy Kidd, who, despite their son's occasional obstreperousness, managed to teach him to love reading.

Thomas Kidd

Contents

Contents

PART TWO

The Documents   29

1. **Jonathan Edwards and the 1735 Northampton
    Revival**   **31**

2. **George Whitefield: The Grand Itinerant**   **43**

3. **Revivals, Conversions, and Spiritual Experiences**   **58**

APPENDIXES

Illustrations

PART ONE

Introduction:
The Contest over
the Great Awakening

On March 7, 1743, James Davenport, one of the most influential leaders of the Great Awakening, removed his pants and cast them into a
bonfire. He called on his followers, gathered on a wharf in New London, Connecticut, to do the same to all their fancy clothes. He believed
their apparel had become barriers blocking their full commitment to
God. The day before, the crowd had burned a pile of books by a variety of Christian authors, and on this day, some in the audience complied with Davenport's exhortation to burn their clothes. Soon "a lofty
pile of hoop petticoats, silk gowns, short cloaks, cambrick caps, red
heeld shoes, fans, necklaces, gloves, and other such aparrell" was fueling the bonfire. For others, however, the call to disrobe crossed a line
of propriety. One particularly bold woman snatched Davenport's pants
from the flames and threw them "into his Face," telling him to come
to his senses. This act broke Davenport's spell over the audience,
who realized that their faith had been transformed into frenzied chaos.
The crowd dispersed, and a contrite Davenport realized he had gone
too far.[1]

This incident, which came at the apex of the First Great Awakening
(the Second Great Awakening occurred during the nineteenth century), raised questions about how to evaluate the series of religious
revivals that had swept through parts of the British colonies in Amer-

ica in the early 1740s. By "revivals" or "awakenings," pastors meant episodes of religious excitement in their congregations that might lead to great numbers of spiritual conversions, in which people would embrace the forgiveness offered to them by Jesus Christ.[2] A huge outbreak of revivals, centered in New England but eventually touching most of the American colonies, began in 1740. Everyone knew that during these awakenings, James Davenport had become among the most successful preachers in New England, but did the bonfire incident, as well as his previous arrests for sedition and slander, mean that the revivals were fundamentally flawed? Were the revivals a legitimate work of God hampered by unfortunate outbreaks of overheated frenzy, or what critics called religious "enthusiasm"? Or did Davenport and others like him pioneer a kind of spiritual democracy, as he routinely led crowds of poor whites, African Americans, and Native Americans singing through the streets of colonial New England?

This book will help you understand why the First Great Awakening of the mid-eighteenth century generated so much excitement and controversy. The Great Awakening was the greatest upheaval in the American colonies prior to the Revolutionary War of the 1770s and 1780s. Historians have usually interpreted the disagreements over the awakenings as a contest between "Old Lights" (those who opposed the revivals) and "New Lights" (those who supported them). As you will see in the documents included here, however, there were really more than two "Lights" during the revivals, as opinions ranged from staunch opposition to tentative support to unmitigated zeal. People could also change their opinions of the revivals very quickly, and some who started out as great supporters became wary of them over time. Overall, there were three main camps during the First Great Awakening: *moderate evangelicals,* who supported the revivals but were deeply concerned about restraining their excesses; *antirevivalists,* who saw the revivals as all emotion and no substance and feared that they would break down the authority of the established ministers; and *radical evangelicals,* who saw the Great Awakening as a new era of spiritual power, accompanied by signs, wonders, and spiritual authority for the common man and woman.[3]

The First Great Awakening, though fraught with disagreements, inaugurated the evangelical movement in American Christianity. Although the word *evangelical* is commonly used today, it is often not clear what the term means. To use a simple definition, *evangelicalism* is a kind of Protestant Christianity that strongly emphasizes the need for personal conversion, or the "new birth." Evangelicals believe that human sin is so offensive to God that it would earn everyone eternal damnation in hell if Jesus had not died on the cross to save people from that punishment. To be saved, however, one must personally receive the forgiveness that Jesus offers. The realization of one's sinfulness, followed by the acceptance of God's mercy, represents the moment of conversion. Although Christians have always emphasized the need for forgiveness through Christ, evangelicals put enormous weight on the individual's decision to accept what Jesus did to save them. At that moment of submission, a sinner is "born again" (a phrase that refers to Jesus's statement in the Gospel of John, chapter 3: "Except a man be born again, he cannot see the kingdom of God"). It is the seminal event of one's life, and the most important—in a sense, the only—goal of evangelical preaching.

Where did evangelical Christianity come from? Many evangelicals would say that it came from Jesus and his apostles. Most historians, however, trace evangelicalism's origins to sources within the European churches of the Protestant Reformation, which began in the early sixteenth century. A number of reformers within Protestantism criticized their own churches for teaching a formal, cold religion instead of a vital, personal relationship with God. In Europe, these "pietistic" groups called on the churches to emphasize "heart religion," not just correct behavior and doctrine.[4] In the American colonies, many European settlers had been influenced by these pietistic movements. Probably the most famous and influential group of pietists in America were the New England Puritans.

Today, the Puritans of colonial New England have developed a popular reputation as dour, mean-spirited persecutors of witches. But many Puritans in England and New England wanted religion to engage the heart and emotions. Some Puritans also accentuated the work of the Holy Spirit in individual Christians' lives. They taught that each Christian had direct access to God through Christ and did not need priests or ministers to intercede for them. Sometimes this could cause trouble for Puritan leaders, as seen in the notorious antinomian controversy of the 1630s, in which laywoman Anne Hutchinson began publicly criticizing the teachings of some pastors in Boston. When she intimated during her trial that she had received her contrarian views from the Holy Spirit, the Puritan judges denounced her as an "antinomian" (one who opposes God's moral law) and banished her from Massachusetts. Hutchinson exemplifies the tendency within Puritanism, and similar kinds of Protestantism in Europe and colonial America, to encourage individualistic interpretation and practice among the laity, even though the Puritans tried to maintain strict religious conformity.

The Puritans had highlighted a person's need for conversion from their beginnings in England, but they tended to see conversion as a long, uncertain process rather than a single event, as an evangelical would. Nevertheless, during periodic "covenant renewals" in seventeenth- and early-eighteenth-century New England, when pastors called on their congregations to recommit to vows they had made to honor God and support the church, large numbers of people often converted at roughly the same time. There were, then, important precedents for the evangelical revivals of the Great Awakening latent in American colonial culture before 1740. But many Puritan leaders undoubtedly emphasized the intellectual content of faith more than emotional experiences, despite their pietistic roots. Similarly, churches before the Great Awakening highly valued order and propriety. Services featured long, formal, and heavily doctrinal sermons read from the pulpit. No one spoke out of turn, and seating was organized by social rank. Despite the maintenance of generally good order, by the late seventeenth century many Puritans had become convinced that New England had entered a period of protracted spiritual decline, as apparent passivity and immorality replaced religious fervor and holiness. Worried pastors wondered whether New Englanders had exchanged true, heartfelt Christian commitment for mere formality and obligatory church attendance.

Many Scots-Irish Presbyterians, who settled in colonial Pennsylvania and New Jersey in large numbers, also focused on the experiential, emotional effects of religious practice. Many came prepared to re-create the so-called "holy fairs" of Scotland and Ulster (Northern Ireland). These regional festivals, centered on large-scale, open-air celebrations of the Lord's Supper (the Christian sacrament of Communion), had for a century stirred the souls of Scots-Irish believers. The Communion season was a fixed feature of Scottish and Scots-Irish Presbyterian practice that would influence the course of the awakenings in North America, as well as the concurrent revivals in Britain. In Scotland, the Great Awakening came to a head at Cambuslang, southeast of Glasgow, where in July and August 1742, major Communion services were celebrated and the popular preacher George Whitefield, recently returned from America, preached to tens of thousands.[5]

Religious and economic difficulties led a number of Ulster Scots to immigrate to North America beginning in the 1710s. Hundreds of thousands of them poured through the Delaware River ports of New

Castle and Philadelphia. Although people from Scotland came in considerable numbers, too, the Ulster Scots dominated the Middle Colonies' Presbyterian church membership rolls. As pastor Samuel Blair wrote in 1744, "All our congregations in Pennsylvania except two or three chiefly are made up of people from [Northern] Ireland."[6]

The Tennent family arrived in Pennsylvania in 1718 amid this flood of Ulster immigrants. William Tennent Sr. and his sons, especially Gilbert, would become the single most influential family in creating Middle Colonies revivalism. They moved to Bucks County, Pennsylvania, and settled in Neshaminy in 1726. Soon after his arrival William Tennent began training candidates for the ministry at the "Log College" seminary. Its graduates helped spread Tennent's style of evangelical preaching throughout the Middle Colonies and also to Virginia.[7]

THE REVIVALS BEGIN

In the 1720s, many pastors began calling for a special outpouring of the Holy Spirit, which would energize the churches and bring about large numbers of conversions, perhaps simultaneously. Everywhere church leaders looked, especially in New England, society seemed threatened with destruction. Native Americans, provoked by unfair treatment by European colonists, periodically attacked frontier settlements, sometimes with the encouragement of the hated French colonists to the north. Often affected by political developments across the Atlantic, the colonists routinely faced dangers from eighteenth-century wars of empire and religion between Protestant Britain and Catholic France and Spain.[8] On the cultural front, colonial colleges had become bastions of theological novelty, which challenged time-honored Protestant doctrines such as predestination (the belief that God chose, or destined, only a fraction of humans to be saved). Traditional pastors, growing ever more desperate for a return to what they saw as the original godly devotion of the colonies, began praying for a new "season of grace" that would turn people's hearts back to God. Whereas older summons for repentance focused on people reforming their own behavior (stopping swearing, drinking, profaning the Sabbath, and so on), now the pastors called on the Holy Spirit to create revivals.[9]

Significant revivals appeared as early as the 1720s in Connecticut, Massachusetts, New Jersey, and Pennsylvania. Gilbert Tennent, ministering in New Brunswick, New Jersey, saw bursts of periodic conversions before the 1740s, as did some of his brothers and other

Presbyterian colleagues, often in conjunction with the emotional open-air Communion services.[10] In New England, a major revival broke out in the Connecticut River valley from 1720 to 1722. In Northampton, Massachusetts, pastor Jonathan Edwards's grandfather and ministerial predecessor Solomon Stoddard led a series of what he called "harvests" in the late seventeenth and early eighteenth centuries, as did Edwards's father, Timothy Edwards, in East Windsor, Connecticut. Stoddard also publicly criticized fellow New England pastors for their dull, uninspired preaching.[11]

The most significant revival in New England before 1734–1735 happened in response to an earthquake that shook the region in 1727. Thomas Prince of the Old South Church in Boston, a future evangelical leader, rejoiced that the terrible shaking had led to a "wonderful Reformation." People had abandoned their grievous sins and had "vastly thronged" the churches. Many hundreds had come forward for baptism, covenant renewal, or admission to Communion. The terror of the earthquake had transformed into the delight of revival. Prince said, "What a Joy is There, even as the Joy of the Harvest, and as Men rejoice when they divide the spoil! What an happy Effusion of the HOLY SPIRIT!"[12]

The revival that historians usually view as the start of the First Great Awakening began in Jonathan Edwards's Northampton church in 1734 (see Document 1). The 1734–1735 Northampton revival commenced among some young people dismayed by the recent deaths of friends. Edwards insisted that the careless youths should consider their state before God and whether they had been born again. The excitement of conversions spread from the youths to adults, and soon the whole community was caught up in the fervor. Many who had been passive about their faith now became intense, committed believers, inspired by their pastor's example. The effects spread throughout the Connecticut River valley, much as the 1720–1722 awakening had. The revival was marked by some exotic spiritual phenomena and behavior, such as divine visions and uproarious laughter during services, but in general the Congregational ministers of New England welcomed the reports of conversions in Northampton. A few New Englanders, such as the non-evangelical Anglican* Timothy Cutler, scoffed at the revival as frenzy (see Document 2). Many non-evangelicals believed that the revivals would open the door to all kinds

---

* Member of the Church of England.

Figure 1. *Jonathan Edwards, 1794*

Jonathan Edwards, pastor of Northampton, Massachusetts, was the greatest theologian to emerge from the Great Awakening. He also led major revivals at his church and defended the awakenings against anti-revivalists' charges that they only represented religious frenzy.

$8.7.23$

A Faithful

NARRATIVE

OF THE

Surprizing Work of GOD

IN THE

CONVERSION

OF

Many HUNDRED SOULS in *Northampton*, and the Neighbouring Towns and Villages of New-*Hampshire* in *New-England*.

In a LETTER to the Rev^d. Dr. BENJAMIN COLMAN of *Boston*.

Written by the Rev^d. Mr. EDWARDS, Minister of *Northampton*, on *Nov.* 6. 1736.

And Published,

With a Large PREFACE,

By Dr. WATTS and Dr. GUYSE.

LONDON;

Printed for JOHN OSWALD, at the *Rose and Crown*, in the *Poultry*, near *Stocks-Market*. M.DCC.XXXVII.

Price stitch'd 1 s. Bound in Calf-Leather, 1 s. 6 d.

of excesses and heresies, fueled by the overheated emotions of individual congregants. Cutler and other opponents of the revivals argued that Christianity thrived on order and structure, not chaos. With the help of Boston ministers, Edwards published *A Faithful Narrative of the Surprising Work of God*, his report on the revival, in London. It established his reputation in Britain as a rising star in the Anglo-American evangelical movement. The vivid description of the awakening also made *A Faithful Narrative* the most influential revival account in the history of evangelicalism.

GEORGE WHITEFIELD: A MEDIA SENSATION

Although Edwards's Northampton revival inaugurated and helped publicize America's part of the Great Awakening, Edwards was not the most important evangelical leader at the time. That role fell to the Anglican priest and itinerant preacher George Whitefield (pronounced "wit-field"), whose extensive travels across the North Atlantic world and celebrated ministry would make him the most famous person in Britain and the colonies, save perhaps for the king. Whitefield, a former stage actor, had been converted at Oxford University in 1735 (see Document 3), partly through the influence of future Methodist leaders John and Charles Wesley. After a mission trip to the new colony of Georgia in 1738, Whitefield returned to England and pioneered his most innovative preaching tactic: the outdoor meeting. In the churches, he was restrained by limited seating capacity and denominational traditions, but in the fields, he could gather as large an audience as possible and focus exclusively on preaching the necessity of the new birth. In England and Wales, Whitefield spoke before gargantuan crowds and became a media star. He used the dramatic techniques of the theater to deliver powerful, emotional sermons that produced thousands of reported conversions. He also adapted strategies of advance publicity and advertising to create excitement in the towns to which he was coming. Whitefield's writings, and even pictures of him,

---

(opposite) **Figure 2.** *Title page of* A Faithful Narrative of the Surprising Work of God, *1737*
First published in London, Jonathan Edwards's *A Faithful Narrative* became the most influential account of a revival from the Great Awakening. It vividly described the conversion experiences of many in the Northampton community.
Beinecke Rare Book and Manuscript Library, Yale University.

Figure 3. *George Whitefield, 1739*
The young Anglican priest George Whitefield was undoubtedly the most important revival preacher of the Great Awakening. He brought his controversial method of "field preaching" from Britain to America in 1739, helping to precipitate the most dramatic phase of the Great Awakening.

By permission of Llyfrgell Genedlaethol Cymru/The National Library of Wales.

became popular sellers for colonial merchants and printers (see Document 6). In late 1739, Whitefield returned to America, where throngs of people welcomed him in towns up and down the Atlantic coast.[13]

Whitefield's example reminds us that the Great Awakening transpired in an Atlantic context. Although no religious leader crossed the ocean as frequently as Whitefield, evangelical ministers actively corresponded with one another and kept tabs on revivals across the Atlantic. In England, Whitefield's colleagues from Oxford, John and Charles Wesley, founded the Methodist movement and brought dramatic change to many Anglican churches. Although the Wesleys eventually broke with Whitefield over theological differences, their focus on conversion and active proselytizing helped expand the evangelical movement in Britain. Wesleyan Methodist itinerant preachers would arrive in America in force after the American Revolution, and by the Civil War, the Methodists were the largest Protestant denomination in the United States.

Despite Whitefield's unprecedented popularity, his 1739 return to America precipitated the forming of battle lines over the revivals. Some observers acknowledged that Whitefield was a powerful preacher but denounced his emotionalism and lack of nuance (see Document 4). His defenders saw him as a great man of God sent to inaugurate new awakenings and large numbers of conversions. Some, like Josiah Smith, Whitefield's chief defender in Charleston, South Carolina, even saw his appearance as the possible fulfillment of prophecy regarding the last days before Christ's return to earth (see Document 5). There is no question that Whitefield's preaching led many to accept Christ's forgiveness personally for the first time. Common farm men and women rushed to see Whitefield preach. For them, attending Whitefield's meetings often was not just about fleeting spiritual ecstasy. Instead his message of turning away from sin and to Christ set their lives on a completely new path (see Documents 9, 10, and 11). Others found it difficult to sustain the excitement of their new life in Christ and fell back into their old ways. Critics reminded evangelicals that frenzied emotions in a revival meeting could not substitute for a lifelong commitment to service and devotion to Christ and the church.

THE AWAKENINGS FLOURISH, 1740–1743

Even after Whitefield returned to Britain, the awakenings in America continued to flourish. Most of the colonies experienced some religious excitement in the early 1740s, but Pennsylvania, New Jersey, Long Island (New York), Connecticut, Rhode Island, and Massachusetts (which at that time included Maine) saw the most activity. Despite the novelty of these commotions, for the Scots-Irish Presbyterians of Pennsylvania and New Jersey, revival still often centered on their great celebrations of Communion (see Document 15). As in Edwards's Northampton awakening, some New England towns seemed totally engulfed by the revival, with women and men, rich and poor, and white, black, and Native American all experiencing the new birth. Edwards continued to play a major role in the 1740s awakenings, highlighted by his famous sermon "Sinners in the Hands of an Angry God," delivered in Enfield, Connecticut, in 1741. In it, Edwards famously warned those who "were never born again" that the "God who holds you over the pit of hell, much as one holds a spider, or some loathsome insect, over the fire, abhors you, and is dreadfully provoked . . . and there is no other reason to be given why you have not dropped into hell since you arose in the morning, but that God's hand has held you up." Delivered before an eager audience, Edwards's sermon fed the spiritual exhilaration churning in the Connecticut River valley, and by the middle of the vivid sermon, congregants had begun screaming for fear of damnation. The staid Edwards decided to stop his address instead of further fueling the conflagration.[14]

Some preachers, such as James Davenport and Daniel Rogers of Ipswich, Massachusetts, seemed to delight in the near anarchy of the meetings (see Document 12). In their revivals, all manner of people spoke of their spiritual experiences and exhorted others to come to Christ. Nowhere else in eighteenth-century America could one see such democratic public speaking, as women, children, African Americans, and Native Americans all addressed the crowds. White men faced the unusual prospect of publicly listening to the words of their social inferiors, yet many white male evangelicals welcomed these new exhorters as brothers and sisters in Christ. The evangelicals' strong emphasis on the empowering effects of the Holy Spirit in every believer tended to level social distinctions in the churches. Earlier in the colonial era, pastors often ruled their churches without question, and only white males with college degrees could become pastors. During the Great Awakening, however, many came to believe that the most important credential for authoritative religious speaking was the indwelling of the Holy Spirit. Some radicals began to recognize common people as exhorters and lay preachers, and some of the most extreme groups, including evangelical Baptists, even ordained uneducated men. Colonial women, Native Americans, and African Americans always had more limited access to public authority, even within the evangelical movement, but some converts, such as Samson Occom, a Mohegan Indian from Connecticut, did receive ordination and became celebrated preachers and missionaries (see Document 10). Likewise, John Marrant, a free African American living in South Carolina, converted after a dramatic encounter with George Whitefield and became a Calvinist Methodist minister in England and Nova Scotia (see Document 17). The First Great Awakening hardly destroyed all social distinctions in or outside of the churches, but it contained the potential to weaken traditional American social hierarchies built on class, race, education, and gender.

SIGNS AND WONDERS

The radical evangelicals pushed hardest against these traditional boundaries, primarily because of their focus on the work of the Holy Spirit in each believer. Their zeal for the Spirit's operations encouraged spiritual phenomena that more moderate observers found frightening and dangerous. Who could tell which of these experiences were legitimate and which were put on for show? Penitents regularly spoke or screamed out during sermons, leading critics to scoff at the evangelicals for being too "noisy." Even moderates often noted that they had to silence congregants who interrupted their sermons during revivals. Moderates gladly welcomed warm responses to their sermons, but they did not want meetings to descend into bedlam. Throughout the records of the Great Awakening, particularly in New England, one also finds regular references to believers experiencing divine dreams, visions, spirit journeys, and trances. Revelations from God did not come from the Bible alone but also from the immediate influence of the Spirit. Sometimes the Spirit chose the most marginal members of society to visit. In Document 13, for instance, an admittedly illiterate correspondent to Connecticut minister Eleazar Wheelock described an incredible journey through heaven and hell. Many reported experiencing such visits to heaven, where angels or Jesus himself showed them whether their name was written in his Book of Life. Others encountered the devil and witnessed the torments of the damned in hell. If the Holy Spirit lived in all believers, and if such phenomena occurred in the New Testament, why couldn't ordinary Christians experience these things, too?[15] Moreover, if lay Christians received such visitations from God and their pastors did not, who was the more spiritually lively and sensitive? These kinds of issues raised questions in the minds of some laypeople about whether their pastors were truly converted.

Recalling the experiences of Anne Hutchinson in the 1630s, laypeople during the Great Awakening demonstrated an amazing capacity to read, interpret, and apply the Scriptures for themselves, sometimes in direct opposition to what their pastors told them. One of the best examples of such lay initiative was the case of Mercy Wheeler, a woman from Plainfield, Connecticut, who had been unable to walk for years (see Document 14). Protestants had conventionally taught that miracles of healing had ceased shortly after the founding era of the ancient Christian church, but Wheeler noticed in the Gospel accounts that Jesus healed people regularly during his earthly ministry. Why, she reasoned, could Jesus not heal her, too? At a 1743 revival meeting, Bible verses about healing flooded her mind, she felt strength surge through her body, and she rose up and began to walk around the room. Shocked critics said that such phenomena should not be expected and that spiritual healing was vastly more important than physical healing. Hostile newspaper commentators even suggested that the miracle was a fake. But according to follow-up reports, Wheeler, who had become a minor star in the evangelical community, maintained her ability to walk for years to come. Not only did she make her own novel application of Scripture, with little apparent pastoral encouragement, but in her healing, she found a venue to become a model of piety in an era when it was very difficult for women to establish any public voice at all.[16]

FRAGMENTATION

Any remaining consensus concerning the revivals began to break down by 1742, partly as a result of the growing controversy over evangelicals' attacks on established clergymen. George Whitefield, Gilbert Tennent, and James Davenport all raised questions about whether established ministers were converted or not. In Tennent's controversial sermon *The Danger of an Unconverted Ministry* (1740), delivered in Nottingham, Pennsylvania, he called unconverted ministers "dead Dogs, that can't bark" and "hireling murderous Hypocrites" (Document 8).[17] Davenport went further than Tennent and even named ministers who he suspected had not experienced the new birth.

These sorts of tactics, and the broader perception that the radical evangelicals were becoming a threat to the established churches, brought down the wrath of New England's provincial governments. Connecticut passed a law forbidding itinerant preachers from entering parishes without the permission of the resident pastor. The law was clearly designed to catch Davenport. The sheriff of Hartford arrested Davenport in May 1742, precipitating a wild courthouse scene described in Document 20. Connecticut authorities expelled the revivalist from the colony, but the effects of his radicalism lingered. For example, radicals set up a training school in New London called the Shepherd's Tent, which drew off zealous students from nearby Yale College.

Hardly chastened by his expulsion from Connecticut, Davenport returned only briefly to his home on Long Island and then set out for Boston. Most of Boston's ministers banned him from preaching in their pulpits; only radicals remained supportive of Davenport. In August 1742, Davenport began publicly identifying ministers he regarded as unconverted, a roster that included several moderate supporters of the awakenings as well as the antirevivalists of Boston. He was arrested and charged with slander. Although a jury voted to convict him, the court reconsidered the matter, declared him insane, and released him.

Davenport returned to Long Island, where he continued to lead heated meetings among his followers. A vision or revelation told him to go back to Connecticut in March 1743. By this time, Davenport had developed an infection in his leg, which may have induced feverish delirium. Based on his previous conduct, however, the book and clothes burning that followed (see Document 22) was no surprise, only a culmination of his meteoric, incendiary career. Immediately after the failed clothes burning, his followers began to abandon him, and Davenport recovered from his leg ailment, only to realize that he risked losing his pastoral career. He began visiting local ministers and apologizing for his behavior. Then, in 1744, he issued his *Confession and Retractions*, a public effort to regain the favor of moderate evangelicals (see Document 23). It affirmed the legitimacy of the awakenings and most of his own work. However, Davenport repudiated his most outlandish actions, especially his antics at the New London bonfire. He attributed that bizarre occasion to the infection in his leg. Although this repentance did not satisfy all critics, Davenport was able to recover his career, but only because he was willing to moderate his style.

DEBATING THE AWAKENINGS

Early in the course of the awakenings, people began to argue about whether and to what extent the new revivals were legitimate works of God. Jonathan Edwards became the revivals' chief defender, despite his reservations about the extremes of Davenport and others. In *The Distinguishing Marks of a Work of the Spirit of God*, delivered at Yale

College's commencement in 1741, Edwards maintained that the emotions displayed at the revival meetings did not determine one way or the other whether the awakenings were legitimate (see Document 18). Instead, he focused on the fruit the excitement produced and believed that if the short-term fervor resulted in more love, generosity, and holiness in the people affected, the revivals were of God. As Edwards grew more moderate over time, he increasingly deemphasized the role of Christians' emotions, fearing that some would substitute external displays for inner transformation of character.

Some people in America took the debates over the Great Awakening to Britain, where Americans desired to maintain a good reputation. In *The State of Religion in New England*, published in Glasgow in 1742, the anonymous A.M. (probably Boston's chief antirevivalist, Charles Chauncy), denounced the revivals and their key leaders (see Document 19). Chauncy adhered to a traditional Puritan model of piety, believing that conversion should be a rational, sober process and that public expressions of emotion added little or nothing to true faith. He elaborated on his opposition to the revivals in his 424-page tome *Seasonable Thoughts on the State of Religion in New England* (1743). He believed that all the revivals would lead inexorably to excesses such as those of Davenport, and he included a litany of these errors as examples. To Chauncy, the churches simply could not operate in a context where long-serving pastors were treated with open contempt and anyone who reported an exotic spiritual experience was revered as a saint. Chauncy's book countered Jonathan Edwards's equally weighty *Some Thoughts concerning the Present Revival of Religion in New England* (1743), which deplored both the deadness of the antirevivalist churches and the chaos of the radicals' meetings, while reaffirming his support for most of the revival activities and the emotions they produced. Historians have rightly regarded the Edwards-Chauncy debate as one of the most important in the Great Awakening, but we should not forget that Edwards did not represent the whole range of evangelical views. The radical evangelicals' leader in New England, Davenport, had little interest in or access to the press. Only a handful of the radicals, led by Davenport's chief defender, Andrew Croswell, published regularly during the Great Awakening. Much of what we know about the radicals actually comes from their opponents.

As a result, radicals, many of whom lacked official ministerial credentials or positions, were largely excluded from the printed debates over the awakenings, giving an undeserved impression of their marginality. Two ministerial conventions in Boston in 1743 tried to issue what appeared to be authoritative evaluations of the revivals, but like the Edwards-Chauncy debate, neither represented the radical position. The first opinion, *The Testimony of the Pastors of the Churches in the Province of the Massachusetts-Bay in New-England,* emerged from a sparsely attended May conference of pastors controlled by a majority of antirevivalists. It focused on the errors of the evangelicals and only grudgingly admitted that signs of real conversions might have appeared in some places. A somewhat larger convention, led mostly by moderate evangelicals, met soon thereafter and issued *The Testimony and Advice of an Assembly of Pastors,* which emphatically affirmed the revivals' authenticity but warned against the radicals' perceived abuses (see Document 21). A group of moderates also insisted on appending a stronger statement against itinerant preaching, or they would not sign the document. Some radical-leaning evangelical ministers did sign *The Testimony and Advice,* but those without an official pastoral position, such as Daniel Rogers, were not allowed to attach their names to it.

The debates over the awakenings culminated in the long-awaited return of George Whitefield to America in late 1744. In 1740, Whitefield had generated an unprecedented stir, but now many pastors turned against him as the source of the radical fractiousness in colonial churches. At least six ministerial associations, along with the faculties of Harvard and Yale (see Document 7), advised ministers not to allow Whitefield access to their pulpits and blamed him for the breakup of a number of churches. Whitefield's critics reminded New Englanders that he, like Davenport, had once openly questioned the salvation of many established pastors. He still had his defenders, however, as represented by the radical-leaning *A Vindication of the Reverend Mr. George Whitefield* (1745), which argued that the itinerant had nothing to be ashamed of regarding his previous work in America. It persisted in suggesting that some of Whitefield's critics might not be converted. Although Whitefield continued to associate openly with radicals, he became more moderate and conciliatory in his style, and he soon regained the favor of most of the clerics, as well as the faculties of Harvard and Yale.

REVIVALS IN THE SOUTH

Most of this survey of the Great Awakening has focused on New England, and for good reason. While the awakenings of 1740 to 1743 did touch most of the colonies, the early Great Awakening's epicenter was clearly in New England. In the South, the early phases were fairly limited in their effects, Whitefield's tours through the coastal South notwithstanding. However, if one sees the Great Awakening as a longer series of developments from the 1740s to the 1780s, and not just a concentrated series of revivals from 1740 to 1743, it becomes easier to integrate the South into the story. Although after 1743 the revivals in America declined until the early nineteenth century, evangelicalism as a movement did not cease to exist, and neither did the evangelicals' desire to promote revivals and mass conversions. Periodic local revivals had become a permanent fixture of the American religious scene, and significant regional awakenings transpired in the early 1760s and throughout the American Revolution. The most important revival of the early 1760s occurred in the Easthampton, Long Island, church of Samuel Buell, who as a young Yale graduate had become an important itinerant preacher in the early 1740s (see Document 16). The southern colonies, where relatively few churches existed, also were alluring targets for many of those ministers touched by the revivals of the early 1740s. By the 1760s, evangelical preachers, many coming from the northern colonies, had begun to traverse the southern backcountry, setting the stage for the widespread growth of evangelical churches there in the nineteenth century.

In the South, to a greater degree than in the North, evangelicals had to confront the issues of race and slavery. In the early stages of the evangelical movement, many key leaders, including Jonathan Edwards, George Whitefield, and James Davenport, were slave owners and were not opposed to slavery per se. However, as seen in Whitefield's admonitory 1740 letter "To the Inhabitants of Maryland, Virginia, North and South-Carolina," white evangelicals did typically insist that slaves be treated well and instructed in Christianity (see Document 24). This frightened many non-evangelical slave masters, who worried that Christianity would make their slaves disobedient. Whitefield, along with many other white evangelicals, assured slave owners that the Bible taught that slaves should obey their masters. Concerns about evangelicalism's effects persisted, however, not least because of the radical behavior of one of Whitefield's early white converts in South Carolina, Hugh Bryan. Bryan was a planter whose conversion under Whitefield's ministry gave him the remarkable idea that he was a prophet chosen to lead slaves out of their captivity (see Document 25). Such intolerable notions led quickly to Bryan's arrest, and Bryan gave up his vision of the slaves' liberation after he tried and failed to part the waters of a local river.[18] Nervousness about evangelicalism's effects continued for a hundred years or more. For example,

Nat Turner's 1831 slave rebellion in Virginia was blamed partly on the influence of radical evangelical ideas among African Americans. Despite white southern evangelicals' general acceptance of slavery, their churches still made inroads among the southern slave population. Scholars have argued that the slaves' interest in evangelical Christianity can be explained by its compatibility with the emotion and musicality of traditional African religions. Also, white evangelicals in the North and South worked hard to bring slaves and free blacks into their churches in a way that dominant southern Anglicans had not. African Americans occasionally found opportunities for leadership in the churches (as exhorters or deacons, though rarely as pastors) and often found that white evangelicals took their spiritual experiences seriously. Enslaved and free African Americans surely found in evangelical faith a source of comfort, dignity, and power—features that also enticed many whites.[19] By the 1750s, significant numbers of African Americans in the South experienced the new birth and joined evangelical congregations. Presbyterian minister Samuel Davies of Virginia, whose views of slavery resembled Whitefield's, described in memorable detail his work among local slaves and their devotion to God (see Document 26).

Yet evangelicals enjoyed their greatest early successes in the South among the isolated and scattered white settlers of the backcountry. As the established state church in the southern colonies, the Church of England received special government support, but its institutional strength rarely extended much beyond coastal cities and towns. Beginning in the 1750s, Presbyterian and Baptist missionaries began seriously to evangelize the backcountry. When the irritable (non-evangelical) Anglican itinerant Charles Woodmason visited the rural Carolinas in the late 1760s, he found the area crawling with evangelicals, who viewed Anglicanism with contempt and regularly harassed the beleaguered missionary (see Document 27). By the time of the Revolution, evangelicals represented only a minority of the southern population, but their quick growth heralded the future transformation of the South into America's "Bible Belt."

SEPARATISTS AND BAPTISTS

In an era when most of the colonies supported one denomination (either Anglican or Congregationalist) as the official state church, nothing could be more disturbing to the establishment than the prospect of church splits and the unauthorized founding of new congregations. Yet as the evangelical movement grew, the criticism of established pastors, especially in New England, often led to such fractures. Ironically, although the Great Awakening strengthened many Americans' personal religious commitment, it also badly damaged the established churches by offering a serious alternative to them. Ultimately, evangelical "dissenters" would lead the charge against all state support for churches. This cause of "disestablishment" gained great traction during the American Revolution.

Early in the Great Awakening, some radicals began breaking away from the state churches, especially in New England, and setting up unauthorized meetings. Eventually, more than a hundred separatist churches sprang up in New England, although many of them did not last long.[20] One of the best examples of church separation occurred in Canterbury, Connecticut, beginning in 1742 (see Documents 30, 31, and 32). In the early 1740s, Canterbury's Congregational church did not have a settled pastor, opening the door for a parade of evangelical itinerants, as well as the exhortations of local brothers Elisha and Solomon Paine, who had no ministerial training. When the church finally received a new pastor, it became evident that he was against the revivals. By 1745, a group of separatists, led by the Paines, formed a new church. Like all such churches, particularly in Connecticut, the Canterbury separatists faced fines and harassment from the government. The separatists especially resented having to pay taxes that went to support the established Congregational church, but their pleas for religious liberty fell on deaf ears.

Some of the radical evangelicals who became separatists went one step further by becoming Baptists. Although Baptists had existed in America since the early colonial period, they remained a fairly small denomination in most areas until the Great Awakening. At that time, some separatists became convinced that the only way to have truly pure churches was to baptize believers following their conversion. Whereas most eighteenth-century Christian denominations in America and Europe practiced infant baptism, the Baptists believed that this practice had no biblical basis. They also worried that infant baptism gave false security to those people baptized as infants who did not experience conversion later in life. The Baptists viewed the ritual of baptism as a symbolic representation of conversion, which could be experienced only by people old enough to understand their sinfulness and their need for the new birth. Almost all of the new Baptists in New England in the mid-eighteenth century came out of the radical/

separatist movement, essentially forming a new evangelical Baptist sect. No one better demonstrated the journey from radical evangelicalism to separatism, and finally to becoming a Baptist, than the great Baptist leader Isaac Backus.

As Backus explains in Document 33, he joined a separatist church in his hometown of Norwich, Connecticut, because he and his fellow radicals perceived that the established church had become corrupt. Although Backus had no college degree, he began to preach in separatist churches and was ordained over a Massachusetts congregation in 1748. Soon Backus came under the influence of Baptists, repudiated infant baptism, and received "believer's baptism" in 1751 (see Document 34). Backus left the separatists and founded a new Baptist church in 1756. Many new evangelicals such as Backus found that the Baptist way fit best with their developing beliefs, and new Baptist churches began springing up across New England in the 1750s and 1760s. Spurred by the zeal of the revivals, some of Backus's New England Baptist colleagues also went as missionaries to the South starting in the 1750s. Two of the first, Shubal Stearns and Daniel Marshall of Connecticut, founded the Sandy Creek Baptist Church in North Carolina in 1755. From Sandy Creek, Baptist missionaries radiated into Virginia and South Carolina. As Charles Woodmason observed in his travels, these Baptists made great inroads into the southern backcountry, where almost no Baptist churches had existed before. Preacher Daniel Fristoe's memoir of a baptismal service in Virginia (see Document 28) shows that the novelty of the Baptists' open-air baptism of adults generated heated emotions and controversy.

Backus became the key advocate for religious liberty in Massachusetts, as he deplored the legal penalties dissenters faced from the Congregationalist establishment. Although the establishment's persecution of dissenters became less severe as the Revolution approached, Backus and other evangelicals seized on the language of liberty used by the patriots to argue that they, too, should enjoy full liberty instead of oppression by New England's colonial governments. In particular, Backus called for freedom to practice Christianity as each person saw fit, with no government penalties or interference (see Document 35). Baptists in Virginia also fought hard for disestablishment, in cooperation with non-evangelicals such as Thomas Jefferson and James Madison. These better-known political leaders based their appeal for religious freedom on principles derived from the Enlightenment, which tended to view organized religion as a foe of social progress. But Baptists such as the minister John Leland were among the most ardent proponents of full religious liberty in Virginia and New England, and they argued that government involvement with religion only hurt the churches (see Document 36). Leland and the Baptists helped secure disestablishment in Virginia in 1786, when Jefferson's Act for Establishing Religious Freedom was passed. Although Massachusetts would be the last state to drop its establishment completely, in the 1830s, one of the most significant political effects of the Great Awakening was to help set the country on a path to disestablishment and the protection of the "free exercise" of religion, as the Constitution's First Amendment, formally adopted in 1791, put it.

HISTORIANS, THE GREAT AWAKENING, AND THE AMERICAN REVOLUTION

In recent decades, historians' interest in the First Great Awakening has grown as evangelical Christianity has played an increasingly public role in modern American life. Historians of eighteenth-century evangelicalism have been concerned with two main issues: first, the effect of the Great Awakening on colonial American society, and second, the Great Awakening's relationship to the American Revolution. On the first issue, historians had, at least since the mid-nineteenth century, taken the importance of the Great Awakening for granted. In 1982, however, historian Jon Butler argued that the Great Awakening was an "interpretative fiction" invented by nineteenth-century evangelicals. According to Butler, the so-called Great Awakening had been limited in scope and had had almost no lasting effects. There really wasn't anything "great" about it.[21]

Although Butler's argument was overstated, it generated an important reevaluation of the Great Awakening and its consequences. Historian Frank Lambert countered that the Great Awakening may have been "invented," but not in the nineteenth century. Instead, it was created by the print media of the 1740s, particularly in the way publishers made George Whitefield into a transatlantic superstar.[22] Other historians have shown how the revivals significantly empowered laypeople, often to the consternation of established ministers and officials.[23]

Butler also dismissed the often suggested idea that the Great Awakening helped drive Americans to revolt against Britain, which is the second main historical topic related to the revivals. Historian Alan Heimert famously argued in *Religion and the American Mind* (1966) that evangelical Calvinism lay at the heart of the "radical, even democratic, social and political ideology" that empowered the Revolution.

Many have rejected his point because the most well-known Founding Fathers were not evangelicals, and because even many non-evangelical ministers enthusiastically supported the Revolution. Secular principles derived from the Enlightenment or republican schools of thought clearly motivated many American revolutionaries, too. Others have supported Heimert's asserted connection between evangelicalism and the Revolution. They contend that evangelicalism likely bred an egalitarian spirit that helped feed a deep social transformation—a democratic revolution in "hearts and minds" accompanying the military and political rebellion.[24]

Some historians have argued that evangelicalism gave the Revolution one of its most potent ideological resources. As historian Philip Greven put it, "Evangelical piety and temperament shaped the political practices of those who were the most ardent republicans." Evangelicalism taught the common people who embraced it that sometimes they must "take matters into their own hands," a subversive tendency that motivated those same people during the imperial crisis, according to historian Gary Nash. The church separations and disruptions of the revivals have been identified by Patricia Bonomi as "a 'practice model' which enabled the provincials to 'rehearse'—though unwittingly—... the arguments ... that would reappear with the political crisis of the 1760s and 1770s." Although such arguments seem plausible, it remains difficult to demonstrate them except by inference. Early evangelicalism, especially in its radical manifestations, could be both spiritually and socially subversive. The evangelical revivals caused the greatest social ferment of any movement prior to the Revolution. This "massive defiance of traditional authority," as historian Gordon Wood called it, must have exercised some shaping influence on the Revolution. Assigning evangelical faith any causal relationship to the Revolution seems implausible, however.[25]

Evangelicalism clearly influenced many patriots' views, giving them a framing vocabulary through which to discuss the imperial crisis. Patriots routinely called Americans back to moral virtuousness and implied that the Revolution had transcendent significance, perhaps even related to the last days before Christ returned to earth. Evangelicals also lent widespread credibility to republican ideology—the faith in human freedom and fear of government corruption that propelled the Revolution. As historian Mark Noll has shown, evangelicals elsewhere in the world largely rejected republicanism, but American evangelicals embraced its "fear of abuses from illegitimate power and ... nearly messianic belief in the benefits of liberty." Some patriots saw a direct link between Christianity and republicanism. As Philadelphia physician Benjamin Rush wrote in 1791, "Republican forms of government are the best repositories of the [Christian] Gospel." Since the 1960s, historians have conclusively demonstrated that these republican ideals fueled the Revolution. Evangelicals championed republicanism as eagerly as other patriots.[26]

As historian Harry Stout has shown, some notable non-evangelical patriots also were shaped by evangelical rhetoric and ideals. Itinerants, led by George Whitefield, gathered audiences of people they did not know and spoke in everyday language filled with biblical allusions. Similarly, many of the leading patriots mobilized the public in the Revolutionary cause by giving simple speeches in everyday language. The informality and anonymity of these sermons and speeches went against the older norms of hierarchy by implicitly endorsing the right of common people to hear, evaluate, and respond to the discourses. Certainly, the patriot assemblies were less participatory, democratic, and inclusive than were many evangelical meetings, but one can still see similarities between them, especially in tactics used by patriot leaders such as Virginia's Patrick Henry, whose "Give me liberty or give me death!" speech was delivered in the style and language of an evangelist.[27]

The connections between the Great Awakening and the Revolution remain indeterminate, but patriots seem to have been conscious of some connection. On September 17, 1775, for instance, Continental army volunteers in Newburyport, Massachusetts, preparing for a campaign against Quebec, attended Sunday services at the town's First Presbyterian Church. First Presbyterian was the final resting place of George Whitefield, who had died in Newburyport on his last visit to America in 1770. After a military procession and church service, some of the officers went down to the crypt and opened Whitefield's tomb. From his decaying body, the men took pieces of his clothes, especially his clerical collar and wristbands. Although they hoped that these relics from an evangelical saint would help them win the battle before them, the mission to Quebec led to a grievous defeat. Even so, in this memorable way, the Continental officers made a connection between evangelicalism and the Revolution.[28]

EVALUATING THE FIRST GREAT AWAKENING AND AMERICAN EVANGELICALISM

Even if the link between the Great Awakening and the Revolution remains a matter of debate, evangelical Christianity retains great significance in American history as one of the most powerful religious movements the country has known. After the Revolution, evangelical Christianity would continue to thrive, despite Thomas Jefferson's confident prediction that all Americans would soon become liberal Unitarians like himself. (Unitarians denied the doctrine of the Trinity and emphasized Jesus's moral teachings over traditional Christian doctrines.) Much to the contrary, evangelical Baptists, Presbyterians, and Methodists grew explosively during the early nineteenth century, as part of what historians conventionally call the Second Great Awakening. By the time of the Civil War, an unusually high percentage of Americans had experienced the new birth. Disestablishment freed America to become more heavily evangelical in its religious and cultural mores. In the Second Great Awakening, new evangelical sects proliferated, and the leadership of the evangelical churches became even more "democratized," as more women, uneducated men, and African Americans found places of power and leadership. Although evangelicals continued to focus on revivals and conversions, evangelicalism was constantly changing. For instance, during the Second Great Awakening, many evangelicals came to reject the doctrines of Calvinism (including predestination) and instead asserted that God gave people the liberty to choose to be saved.[29]

After the Civil War, America became increasingly diverse in its religious practices. Following the Scopes trial, which focused the nation's attention on the teaching of evolutionary theory in public schools in 1925, "fundamentalist" Christianity seemed to go underground for several decades. But with the arrival of globe-trotting evangelist Billy Graham in the 1950s and the rise of the Religious Right in the 1970s, evangelical Christianity returned in force. Today, evangelical Christianity in America is "embattled and thriving," to use sociologist Christian Smith's phrase. In other words, evangelicals in America seem to do best when they perceive themselves as being in cultural or religious crisis. Even though eighteenth-century evangelicals lived in a very different cultural context—we should not imagine that there is a straight line connecting George Whitefield to Billy Graham—they had a similar sense of battling established churches, ministers, and sometimes governments.[30] The recent global explosion of evangelicalism, and the related movement of Pentecostalism, has fundamentally shifted the nature of world Christianity. Much larger numbers of people are converting to Christianity in the Southern Hemisphere than in its traditional northern centers of strength, especially western Europe.[31] Yet many evangelicals around the globe still look to America's First Great Awakening as an important beginning. In 1997, for instance, Jonathan Edwards's *A Faithful Narrative* was translated into

Korean, following many earlier non-English translations of that most influential text. To study the First Great Awakening, then, is to examine the early history of a movement that continues to have a great deal of contemporary relevance.

NOTES

[1] Robert W. Brockway, *A Wonderful Work of God: Puritanism and the Great Awakening* (Bethlehem, Pa.: Lehigh University Press, 2003), 148–49.

[2] Christopher Grasso, *A Speaking Aristocracy: Transforming Public Discourse in Eighteenth-Century Connecticut* (Chapel Hill: University of North Carolina Press, 1999), 89.

[3] Much of this introduction is based on material from my forthcoming book, *The Great Awakening: The Roots of Evangelical Christianity in Colonial America* (New Haven, Conn.: Yale University Press). Fuller documentation and elaboration can be found there.

[4] Ted Campbell, *The Religion of the Heart: A Study of European Religious Life in the Seventeenth and Eighteenth Centuries* (Columbia: University of South Carolina Press, 1991).

[5] Leigh Eric Schmidt, *Holy Fairs: Scotland and the Making of American Revivalism*, 2nd ed. (Grand Rapids, Mich.: Eerdmans, 2001), 3.

[6] Marilyn J. Westerkamp, *The Triumph of the Laity: Scots-Irish Piety and the Great Awakening, 1625–1760* (New York: Oxford University Press, 1988), 142.

[7] Ibid., 167; Milton J. Coalter Jr., *Gilbert Tennent, Son of Thunder: A Case Study of Continental Pietism's Impact on the First Great Awakening in the Middle Colonies* (Westport, Conn.: Greenwood Press, 1986), 1–5.

[8] Thomas S. Kidd, *The Protestant Interest: New England after Puritanism* (New Haven, Conn.: Yale University Press, 2004).

[9] Michael J. Crawford, *Seasons of Grace: Colonial New England's Revival Tradition in Its British Context* (New York: Oxford University Press, 1991).

[10] Coalter, *Gilbert Tennent*, 38–54.

[11] George M. Marsden, *Jonathan Edwards: A Life* (New Haven, Conn.: Yale University Press, 2003), 25.

[12] Thomas Prince, *Earthquakes the Works of God*, 2nd ed. (Boston, 1727), appendix.

[13] Frank Lambert, *"Pedlar in Divinity": George Whitefield and the Transatlantic Revivals, 1737–1770* (Princeton, N.J.: Princeton University Press, 1994); Harry S. Stout, *The Divine Dramatist: George Whitefield and the Rise of Modern Evangelicalism* (Grand Rapids, Mich.: Eerdmans, 1991).

[14] Jonathan Edwards, "Sinners in the Hands of an Angry God," in *The Sermons of Jonathan Edwards: A Reader*, ed. Wilson H. Kimnach, Kenneth P. Minkema, and Douglas A. Sweeney (New Haven, Conn.: Yale University Press, 1999), 57–58; Douglas L. Winiarski, "Jonathan Edwards, Enthusiast? Radical Revivalism and the Great Awakening in the Connecticut Valley," *Church History*, 74, no. 4 (December 2005): 683–739.

[15] Douglas L. Winiarski, "Souls Filled with Ravishing Transport: Heavenly Visions and the Radical Awakening in New England," *William and Mary Quarterly*, 3rd ser., 61, no. 1 (January 2004): 3–46.

[16] Thomas S. Kidd, "The Healing of Mercy Wheeler: Illness and Miracles among Early American Evangelicals," *William and Mary Quarterly*, 3rd ser., 63, no. 1 (January 2006): 149–70.

[17] Gilbert Tennent, "The Danger of an Unconverted Ministry," in *The Great Awakening: Documents Illustrating the Crisis and Its Consequences*, ed. Alan Heimert and Perry Miller (Indianapolis: Bobbs-Merrill, 1967), 80, 83.

[18] Harvey H. Jackson, "Hugh Bryan and the Evangelical Movement in Colonial South Carolina," *William and Mary Quarterly*, 3rd ser., 43, no. 4 (October 1986): 594–614.

[19] Erik Seeman, "'Justise Must Take Plase': Three African Americans Speak of Religion in Eighteenth-Century New England," *William and Mary Quarterly*, 3rd ser., 56, no. 2 (April 1999): 395–96; Sylvia R. Frey and Betty Wood, *Come Shouting to Zion: African American Protestantism in the American South and British Caribbean to 1830* (Chapel Hill: University of North Carolina Press, 1998).

[20] C. C. Goen, *Revivalism and Separatism in New England, 1740–1800: Strict Congregationalists and Separate Baptists in the Great Awakening*, rev. ed. (Middletown, Conn.: Wesleyan University Press, 1987).

[21] Jon Butler, "Enthusiasm Described and Decried: The Great Awakening as Interpretative Fiction," *Journal of American History*, 69, no. 2 (September 1982): 305–25.

[22] Frank Lambert, *Inventing the "Great Awakening"* (Princeton, N.J.: Princeton University Press, 1999).

[23] See, for example, Rhys Isaac, *The Transformation of Virginia, 1740–1790* (Chapel Hill: University of North Carolina Press, 1982); Westerkamp, *The Triumph of the Laity*; Winiarski, "Souls Filled with Ravishing Transport."

[24] Alan Heimert, *Religion and the American Mind: From the Great Awakening to the Revolution* (Cambridge, Mass.: Harvard University Press, 1966), viii.

[25] Philip Greven, *The Protestant Temperament: Patterns of Child-Rearing, Religious Experience, and the Self in Early America* (Chicago: University of Chicago Press, 1977), 354; Gary Nash, *The Urban Crucible: The Northern Seaports and the Origins of the American Revolution*, abr. ed. (Cambridge, Mass.: Harvard University Press, 1986), 135–36; Patricia Bonomi, *Under the Cope of Heaven: Religion, Society, and Politics in Colonial America* (New York: Oxford University Pres, 1986), 153; Gordon S. Wood, "Religion and the American Revolution," in *New Directions in American Religious History*, ed. Harry S. Stout and D. G. Hart (New York: Oxford University Press, 1997), 182.

[26] Mark A. Noll, *America's God: From Jonathan Edwards to Abraham Lincoln* (New York: Oxford University Press, 2002), 56; Benjamin Rush to Elhanan Winchester, November 12, 1791, quoted in ibid., 65. Classic histories of republicanism in America include Bernard Bailyn, *The Ideological Origins of the American Revolution* (Cambridge, Mass.: Harvard University Press, 1967); Gordon Wood, *The Creation of the American Republic, 1776–1787* (Chapel Hill: University of North Carolina Press, 1967); Gordon Wood, *The Radicalism of the American Revolution* (New York: Knopf, 1992).

[27] Harry S. Stout, "Religion, Communications, and the Ideological Origins of the American Revolution," *William and Mary Quarterly*, 3rd ser., 34, no. 4 (October 1977): 519–41; Isaac, *Transformation of Virginia*, 265–67.

[28] Charles Royster, *A Revolutionary People at War: The Continental Army and American Character, 1775–1783* (Chapel Hill: University of North Carolina Press, 1979), 23–24; Heimert, *Religion and the American Mind*, 483.

[29] Nathan O. Hatch, *The Democratization of American Christianity* (New Haven, Conn.: Yale University Press, 1989).

[30] Christian Smith, *American Evangelicalism: Embattled and Thriving* (Chicago: University of Chicago Press, 1998).

[31] Philip Jenkins, *The Next Christendom: The Coming of Global Christianity* (New York: Oxford University Press, 2003).

PART TWO

The Documents

1

Jonathan Edwards and the
1735 Northampton Revival

1

JONATHAN EDWARDS

A Faithful Narrative

1737

Jonathan Edwards (1703–1758) was the most influential theologian in early America. He also led important revivals during the Great Awakening, including the first, which happened in Edwards's Northampton, Massachusetts, church in 1734–1735. It would become the most famous revival in Christian history. In A Faithful Narrative of the Surprising Work of God, *Edwards described for a British and American audience what happened.*

At the latter end of the year 1733, there appeared a very unusual flexibleness, and yielding to advice, in our young people. It had been too long their manner to make the evening after the Sabbath, and after our public lecture,[1] to be especially the times of their mirth and company-keeping. But a sermon was now preached on the Sabbath before the lecture, to shew the evil tendency of the practice, and to persuade

---

[1]A minister's "lecture" was regularly given on a weekday, while his "sermon" was given on Sunday.

From Jonathan Edwards, *A Faithful Narrative of the Surprising Work of God*, in *The Great Awakening*, vol. 4, *The Works of Jonathan Edwards*, ed. C. C. Goen (New Haven, Conn.: Yale University Press, 1972), 147–210.

them to reform it; and it was urged on heads of families, that it should be a thing agreed upon among them, to govern their families and keep their children at home at these times; and withal it was more privately moved that they should meet together the next day, in their several neighborhoods, to know each other's minds; which was accordingly done, and the motion complied with throughout the town. But parents found little or no occasion for the exercise of government in the case: the young people declared themselves convinced by what they had heard from the pulpit, and were willing of themselves to comply with the counsel that had been given: and it was immediately, and I suppose, almost universally complied with; and there was a thorough reformation of these disorders thenceforward, which has continued ever since.

Presently after this, there began to appear a remarkable religious concern at a little village belonging to the congregation, called Pascommuck, where a few families were settled at about three miles distance from the main body of the town. At this place, a number of persons seemed to be savingly wrought upon. In the April following, *anno*[2] 1734, there happened a very sudden and awful death of a young man in the bloom of his youth; who being violently seized with a pleurisy and taken immediately very delirious, died in about two days; which (together with what was preached publicly on that occasion) much affected many young people. This was followed with another death of a young married woman, who had been considerably exercised in mind about the salvation of her soul before she was ill, and was in great distress in the beginning of her illness; but seemed to have satisfying evidences of God's saving mercy to her before her death; so that she died very full of comfort, in a most earnest and moving manner warning and counseling others. This seemed much to contribute to the solemnizing of the spirits of many young persons: and there began evidently to appear more of a religious concern on people's minds.

In the fall of that year, I proposed it to the young people, that they should agree among themselves to spend the evenings after lectures in social religion,[3] and to that end divide themselves into several companies to meet in various parts of the town; which was accordingly done, and those meetings have been since continued, the example imitated by elder people. This was followed with the death of an elderly

---

[2] In the year.
[3] Conversations about religion in small groups.

person, which was attended with many unusual circumstances, by which many were much moved and affected. . . .

. . . And then it was, in the latter part of December, that the Spirit of God began extraordinarily to set in, and wonderfully to work amongst us; and there were, very suddenly, one after another, five or six persons who were to all appearance savingly converted, and some of them wrought upon in a very remarkable manner.

Particularly, I was surprised with the relation of a young woman, who had been one of the greatest company-keepers in the whole town. When she came to me, I had never heard that she was become in any wise serious, but by the conversation I then had with her, it appeared to me that what she gave an account of was a glorious work of God's infinite power and sovereign grace; and that God had given her a new heart, truly broken and sanctified. I could not then doubt of it, and have seen much in my acquaintance with her since to confirm it.

Though the work was glorious, yet I was filled with concern about the effect it might have upon others: I was ready to conclude (though too rashly) that some would be hardened by it, in carelessness and looseness of life; and would take occasion from it to open their mouths in reproaches of religion. But the event was the reverse, to a wonderful degree; God made it, I suppose, the greatest occasion of awakening to others, of anything that ever came to pass in the town. I have had abundant opportunity to know the effect it had, by my private conversation with many. The news of it seemed to be almost like a flash of lightning, upon the hearts of young people all over the town, and upon many others. Those persons amongst us who used to be farthest from seriousness, and that I most feared would make an ill improvement of it, seemed greatly to be awakened with it; many went to talk with her, concerning what she had met with; and what appeared in her seemed to be the satisfaction of all that did so.

Presently upon this, a great and earnest concern about the great things of religion and the eternal world became universal in all parts of the town, and among persons of all degrees and all ages; the noise amongst the dry bones[4] waxed louder and louder. All other talk about spiritual and eternal things was soon thrown by; all the conversation in all companies and upon all occasions, was upon these things only, unless so much as was necessary for people, carrying on their ordinary secular business. Other discourse than of the things of religion would scarcely be tolerated in any company. The minds of people

---

[4]A reference to Ezekiel 37.

were wonderfully taken off from the world; it was treated amongst us as a thing of very little consequence. They seemed to follow their worldly business more as a part of their duty than from any disposition they had to it; the temptation now seemed to lie on that hand, to neglect worldly affairs too much, and to spend too much time in the immediate exercise of religion: which thing was exceedingly misrepresented by reports that were spread in distant parts of the land, as though the people here had wholly thrown by[5] all worldly business, and betook themselves entirely to reading, and praying, and such like religious exercises.

But although people did not ordinarily neglect their worldly business; yet there then was the reverse of what commonly is: religion was with all sorts the great concern, and the world was a thing only by the bye. The only thing in their view was to get the kingdom of heaven, and everyone appeared pressing into it. The engagedness of their hearts in this great concern could not be hid; it appeared in their very countenances. It then was a dreadful thing amongst us to lie out of Christ, in danger every day of dropping into hell; and what persons' minds were intent upon was to escape for their lives, and to fly from the wrath to come.[6] All would eagerly lay hold of opportunities for their souls; and were wont very often to meet together in private houses for religious purposes: and such meetings when appointed were wont greatly to be thronged.

There was scarcely a single person in the town, either old or young, that was left unconcerned about the great things of the eternal world. Those that were wont to be the vainest and loosest, and those that had been most disposed to think and speak slightly of vital and experimental religion, were now generally subject to great awakenings. And the work of conversion was carried on in a most astonishing manner, and increased more and more; souls did as it were come by flocks to Jesus Christ. From day to day, for many months together, might be seen evident instances of sinners brought out of darkness into marvellous light, and delivered out of an horrible pit, and from the miry clay, and set upon a rock with a new song of praise to God in their mouths.

This work of God, as it was carried on, and the number of true saints multiplied, soon made a glorious alteration in the town; so that in the spring and summer following, *anno* 1735, the town seemed to be full of the presence of God: it never was so full of love, nor so full of

---

[5] Abandoned.
[6] God's judgment against sinners.

joy; and yet so full of distress, as it was then. There were remarkable tokens of God's presence in almost every house. It was a time of joy in families on the account of salvation's being brought unto them; parents rejoicing over their children as newborn, and husbands over their wives, and wives over their husbands. The goings of God were then seen in his sanctuary, God's day was a delight, and his tabernacles were amiable. Our public assemblies were then beautiful; the congregation was alive in God's service, everyone earnestly intent on the public worship, every hearer eager to drink in the words of the minister as they came from his mouth; the assembly in general were, from time to time, in tears while the word was preached: some weeping with sorrow and distress, others with joy and love, others with pity and concern for the souls of their neighbors.

Our public praises were then greatly enlivened; God was then served in our psalmody, in some measure, in the beauty of holiness. It has been observable that there has been scarce any part of divine worship, wherein good men amongst us have had grace so drawn forth and their hearts so lifted up in the ways of God, as in singing his praises. Our congregation excelled all that ever I knew in the external part of the duty before, generally carrying regularly and well three parts of music, and the women a part by themselves. But now they were evidently wont to sing with unusual elevation of heart and voice, which made the duty pleasant indeed. . . .

This has also appeared to be a very extraordinary dispensation, in that the Spirit of God has so much extended not only his awakening but regenerating influences, both to elderly persons and also those that are very young. It has been a thing heretofore rarely to be heard of, that any were converted past middle age; but now we have the same around to think that many such have in this time been savingly changed, as that others have been so in more early years. I suppose there were [converted] upwards of fifty persons in this town above forty years of age; and more than twenty of them above fifty, and about ten of them above sixty, and two of them above seventy years of age.

It has heretofore been looked on as a strange thing, when any have seemed to be savingly wrought upon, and remarkably changed in their childhood; but now, I suppose, near thirty were to appearance so wrought upon between ten and fourteen years of age, and two between nine and ten, and one of about four years of age. . . . The influences of God's Spirit have also been very remarkable on children in some other places, particularly at Sunderland and South Hadley, and the west part of Suffield.[7] There are several families in this town that are all hopefully pious; yea, there are several numerous families in which, I think, we have reason to hope that all the children are truly godly, and most of them lately become so: and there are very few houses in the whole town into which salvation has not lately come, in one or more instances. There are several Negroes, that from what was seen in them then, and what is discernible in them since, appear to have been truly born again in the late remarkable season.

God has also seemed to have gone out of his usual way in the quickness of his work, and the swift progress his Spirit has made in his operations on the hearts of many. 'Tis wonderful that persons should be so suddenly, and yet so greatly, changed: many have been taken from a loose and careless way of living, and seized with strong convictions of their guilt and misery, and in a very little time "old things have passed away, and all things have become new with them."[8]

God's work has also appeared very extraordinary in the degrees of the influences of his Spirit, both in the degree of awakening, and conviction,[9] and also in the degree of saving light, and love, and joy, that many have experienced. It has also been very extraordinary in the extent of it, and its being so swiftly propagated from town to town. In former times of the pouring out of the Spirit of God on this town, though in some of them it was very remarkable, yet it reached no further than this town; the neighboring towns all around continued unmoved. . . .

Persons commonly at first conversion and afterwards, have had many texts of Scripture brought to their minds, that are exceeding suitable to their circumstances, which often come with great power, and as the Word of God or Christ indeed: and many have a multitude of sweet invitations, promises, and doxologies[10] flowing in one after another, bringing great light and comfort with them, filling the soul brimful, enlarging the heart. and opening the mouth in religion. And it seems to me necessary to suppose, that there is an immediate influence of the Spirit of God, oftentimes in bringing texts of Scripture to the mind: not that I suppose 'tis done in a way of immediate revelation, without any manner of use of the memory; but yet there seems plainly to be an immediate and extraordinary influence, in leading their

[7] Nearby towns.
[8] 2 Corinthians 5:17.
[9] Of sin.
[10] Hymns of praise to God.

thoughts to such and such passages of Scripture, and exciting them in the memory. Indeed in some God seems to bring texts of Scripture to their minds no otherwise than by leading them into such frames and mediations, as harmonize with those Scriptures; but in many persons there seems to be something more than this. . . .

Many in the country have entertained a mean thought of this great work that there has been amongst us, from what they have heard of impressions that have been made on persons' imaginations. But there have been exceeding great misrepresentations and innumerable false reports concerning that matter. 'Tis not, that I know of, the profession or opinion of any one person in the town, that my weight is to be laid on anything seen with the bodily eyes: I know the contrary to be a received and established principle amongst us. I cannot say that there have been no instances of persons that have been ready to give too much heed to vain and useless imaginations; but they have been easily corrected, and I conclude it will not be wondered at, that a congregation should need a guide in such cases, to assist them in distinguishing wheat from chaff.[11] But such impressions on the imagination as have been more usual, seem to me to be plainly no other than what is to be expected in human nature in such circumstances, and what is the natural result of the strong exercise of the mind, and impressions on the heart.

I do not suppose that they themselves imagined that they saw anything with their bodily eyes; but only have had within them ideas strongly impressed, and as it were, lively pictures in their minds: as for instance, some when in great terrors, through fear of hell, have had lively ideas of a dreadful furnace. Some, when their hearts have been strongly impressed, and their affections greatly moved with a sense of the beauty and excellency of Christ, it has wrought on their imaginations so, that together with a sense of his glorious spiritual perfections, there has arisen in the mind an idea of one of glorious majesty, and of a sweet and a gracious aspect. So some, when they have been greatly affected with Christ's death, have at the same time a lively idea of Christ hanging upon the cross, and of his blood running from his wounds; which things won't be wondered at by them that have observed how strong affections about temporal matters will excite lively ideas and pictures of different things in the mind. . . .

---

[11]Seed coverings of wheat removed by threshing; a reference to Matthew 3:12 and Luke 3:17.

... God has so ordered the manner of the work in many respects, as very signally and remarkably to shew it to be his own peculiar and immediate work, and to secure the glory of it wholly to his almighty power and sovereign grace. And whatever the circumstances and means have been, and though we are so unworthy, yet so hath it pleased God to work! And we are evidently a people blessed of the Lord! And here, in this corner of the world, God dwells and manifests his glory.

2

TIMOTHY CUTLER

Critique of the Northampton Awakening

1739

Timothy Cutler (1684–1765) did not think highly of the Northampton awakening. Cutler had shocked New England's Congregationalists in 1722 when, as the rector of Yale College, he publicly converted to Anglicanism. Yale was a Congregationalist college, and Cutler's conversion to the maligned Anglican denomination caused much consternation. (Although George Whitefield was an Anglican, he was unusual in his interdenominational cooperation.) Cutler soon became the key Anglican leader in New England. In the 1739 letter to the Anglican bishop of London excerpted here, Cutler portrayed the Northampton awakening as religious fanaticism. In the second part of the letter, he explained his fear that the Northampton revival was making children wild and disobedient to their parents and, in the worst cases, causing some people to commit suicide out of hysteria and despair.

My Lord, I am personally acquainted with Mr Edwards of Northampton, who is now in Town, and has made me a Visit: but as I expected

From Douglas C. Stenerson, ed., "An Anglican Critique of the Early Phase of the Great Awakening in New England: A Letter by Timothy Cutler," *William and Mary Quarterly*, 3rd ser., 30, no. 3 (July 1973): 480–87.

no more light from Him than what his Book[1] contain'd, we kept clear of that Subject. Nor was I an entire Stranger to his Grandfather, Mr Solomon Stoddard, his Predecessor there. . . .

Mr Edwards was brought up under my care at Yale College, a Person of good Abilities, Diligence, and Proficiency in Learning, and continues his application [t]o this time, and in such a degree, that He is very much emaciated, and impair'd in his Health, and it is doubtful to me whether He will attain to the Age of 40.[2] He was Critical, subtil and peculiar, but I think not very solid in Disputation. Always a sober Person, but withal pretty recluse, austere and rigid. Presently after He left the College, He remo[v]ed to Northampton to assist his Grandfather, and was intirely formed by Him, and now has the care of a People at a great distance from the promiscuous Conversation and the Infection of our Sea-ports, generally regular and sober, uniform in Sentiment but remarkably train'd up in self conceit, to Disputation, and a Fondness for Mr Stoddard's own school-Divinity.

About the time of this remarkable Appearance at Northampton and the parts adjacent, there was a number of Visionaries at Cambridge, and in the College there.[3] It began in one Langloiserie,[4] a Refugee from Canada, who dwell't in Cambridge to teach the Scholars French, and insinuated himself into the Esteem of many, by a sober Life, and demure Behavior mixed with much Enthusiasm,[5] tho' He refuses to attend any Public Worship, and has privately discovered, and laboured to propagate gross Corruptions in Religion. He is report[ed] [to] be an Arian,[6] to believe two Messiahs, Ben David and Ben Ephraim,[7] and to have given out that the World would come to an end within a year or two of that time. One of the Tutors of the College, with several of His Relations, who are Teachers, appeared much affected by it, and remarkably careless about Temporal Affairs; at which the College was alarmed, and warned the Scholar[s] against any Conversation with this Langloiserie, and brought the Tutor of the College to some Reflections; and so this matter stopt there. But the Perswasion that the World would soon come to an end got up to Northampton-parts, and

---

[1] *A Faithful Narrative of the Surprising Work of God* (see Document 1).
[2] Edwards was thirty-six at the time.
[3] Harvard College.
[4] Louis l'Angloiserie, a French instructor at Harvard.
[5] Overzealous religious passion.
[6] One who does not believe that God the Father and God the Son (Jesus) are equal.
[7] An obscure belief that there would be two Messiahs: Messiah ben David (Jesus) and a secondary Messiah, ben Ephraim, to precede him.

wrought much on the People's Spirits, and what engaged the Indians thereabouts I cannot tell, but are also said to have at that time conversed with the English more seriously, and to have been more abstemious than was common for them. . . .

. . . Tho' a few that I have spoken with give in to the Truth of the Narrative: but all say that it is now over, and generally add, that many are become as bad as ever.

Several inform me, That their Imaginations were much wrought [on,] some pretending to have seen very strange Sights, some surprizing Lights, and one an Hawk on a Stump of a Tree. A Friend of mine who travelled into thos[e] parts asked a Teacher there, whether *He thought the thing was not catching*? who answered He did. Another Teacher of those parts, and a very worthy sensible man[,] told me upon Enquiry formerly, That He thought there was something remarkable in it, but it was too much magnify'd and strain'd, and proposed to give me a visit, and to discourse more upon the Subject, but I was disappointed. I have since written to Him upon it, and received no answer, but know not why, unless that He is [s]hy at this juncture, being hotly charged with Arminianism.[8] A Preacher said He had two Sisters who had *gone through the work* (a favourite Phrase on the Subject) but they were no better than before. I laboured to gain a Visit from Him but that stirred up his Jealousy, and He will not see me. A man of Hatfield says, His Minister Mr Wm. Williams, (tho' He is one that attests the Narrative) wishes Mr Edwards had not been so full and forward in the matter, and I have no rea[son] t[o] doubt it, because such things are frequently hurryed on among us by an in[j]udicious Zeal, and it is scandalous to be slack and deliberate, and because good information perswades me He is a very honest man: He also thinks there is [not] [s]o much in it as is pretended, but is glad He did not see me, as I laid out for it. From others I find that Children of about 12 years old would run about the streets, and say, they were *bound to Zion*,[9] and would *enquire the way Zion ward*, that they would assemble to pray and sing in the Meeting-houses, and were admitted to the Communion, that the Height of this Paroxysm was within two Months, and as all others say, now for a considerable time entirely over; and that the sober Anabaptists[10] in those parts take it for a whim,

[8]Arminians believed, against Calvinism, that God gave people free will to choose to be saved or not. Most eighteenth-century American evangelicals were Calvinists.
[9]Heaven.
[10]Baptists.

and sundry others question the nature and tendency of the thing, but conceal themselves for fear of Displeasure.

It is credibly reported by sundry, That one Mr Hawley hanged himself at this time, because what He had been seeking for, and had not found in fourty years, others had found in a few days, and that another cut his Throat upon it, but the Wound proved not mortal.[11]

I employed a Dissenting Friend of mine in this Town to assist my Enquiries; and He finds two Persons who have studiously examin'd the matter. The one is a Teacher, who finds it had its Rise from a Report that the World would [p]resently come to an end, strengthened by Mr Whiston's Prediction of a Comet,[12] that many of the Converts have relapsed, and He thinks there is nothing in it: Another is a very consciencious discreet Dissenter,[13] greatly reverencing and respectful towards his Teachers, and whom I should rather expect to fall into the Scheme than not. He, after strict Enquiry cannot find the Rise to be from Preaching, or any thing Providential; He thinks there were good Impressions among some, but *much chaff among the wheat.* And He reports this Story as very credible: A Certain Person in Northampton wanted [to] supply his Pile of Firewood, which was low, and bad[14] his son go into the Woods and [g]et some Firewood, who said *He could not.* Whereupon his Father argued with Him, and bad him observe the need they were under; but He continued saying [*H*]*e could not go.* At length his Father told Him that unless He was ill, He would [p]ut forth his Authority, and make Him go. And then his Son took up his Ax and went into the Barn, where He made an hideous Mourning and Noise, that [a]larm'd the Neighbours and they went to Him, and then called his Father. At [l]ength it was moved to send for Mr Edwards their Minister before whom He conti[n]ued in this manner, who thereupon advised the Father to forbear urging his [S]on, telling Him that He was under some extraordinary Influence of the [S]pirit, and was *getting through*: a Phrase much apply'd to such cases.

Upon the whole, My Lord, I find it to be the sence of People in general [t]hat in this great Appearance of Religion there is reason to think

---

[11]Cutler was confused regarding the details of these suicides. Edwards's uncle Joseph Hawley, apparently distressed because he feared his own damnation to hell, successfully committed suicide by cutting his throat. Thomas Stebbins, also of Northampton, attempted to cut his throat but did not kill himself.

[12]William Whiston's *A New Theory of the Earth* (London: 1696) speculated that the earth would be destroyed by a comet.

[13]An Anglican term for English Protestants not affiliated with the Anglican Church.

[14]Told.

many were real, [t]hat others were led by Example, that many remain serious and unblemisht, and [p]erhaps as many who were bad have relapsed in to their former state; and that People in those parts anything unbyast[15] by their popular Schemes, think there was [a] great deal fantastical and foolish in those shows, but find it not for their [in]terest to speak disparagingly of them; that the meanest of the Teachers, here and there, and scarce any other Teachers, fall into them; and that the Talk of these [th]ings is now generally dropt.

[15] Objective.

2

George Whitefield:
The Grand Itinerant

3

GEORGE WHITEFIELD

Journals
1735–1740

George Whitefield (1714–1770) was the most important itinerant, or touring evangelist, of the First Great Awakening. The young Anglican minister electrified crowds in Britain and America with his dramatic preaching style. He successfully publicized his tours through the use of the press, and his autobiographical Journals *became bestsellers on both sides of the Atlantic. In these selections, Whitefield describes his early life at Oxford University, where poor eating and sleeping habits made him sick and emaciated. After his dramatic conversion experience, he began his preaching ministry in Britain and America. The distinctive features of Whitefield's work were outdoor assemblies and his single-minded focus on the new birth of salvation. Although Whitefield surely exaggerated the size of his audiences, he undoubtedly drew throngs of people wherever he went. At these meetings, Whitefield passionately insisted that everyone needed to accept Christ's free offer of forgiveness and be born again.*

Whitefield's unusual belief in interdenominational cooperation was evident in his confrontation with Timothy Cutler (author of Document 2), the Anglican commissary of Boston. In an age when advocates

From George Whitefield, *George Whitefield's Journals* (Carlisle, Pa.: Banner of Truth Trust, 1960), 57–58, 215–16, 276–77, 457–62, 487.

of different religious denominations often regarded one another with contempt, Whitefield believed that he could work with any Christian who believed in the new birth. Cutler did not consider as legitimate ministers and churches outside the Anglican fold.

This fit of sickness continued upon me for seven weeks, and a glorious visitation it was. The blessed Spirit was all this time purifying my soul. All my former gross and notorious, and even my heart sins[1] also, were now set home upon me, of which I wrote down some remembrance immediately, and confessed them before God morning and evening. Though weak, I often spent two hours in my evening retirements, and prayed over my Greek Testament and Bishop Hall's[2] most excellent *Contemplations*, every hour that my health would permit. About the end of the seven weeks, and after I had been groaning under an unspeakable pressure both of body and mind for above a twelve-month, God was pleased to set me free in the following manner. One day, perceiving an uncommon drought and a disagreeable clamminess in my mouth and using things to allay my thirst, but in vain, it was suggested to me, that when Jesus Christ cried out, "I thirst,"[3] His sufferings were near at an end. Upon which I cast myself down on the bed, crying out, "I thirst! I thirst!" Soon after this, I found and felt in myself that I was delivered from the burden that had so heavily oppressed me. The spirit of mourning was taken from me, and I knew what it was truly to rejoice in God my Saviour; and, for some time, could not avoid singing psalms wherever I was; but my joy gradually became more settled, and, blessed be God, has abode and increased in my soul, saving a few casual intermissions, ever since.

Thus were the days of my mourning ended. After a long night of desertion and temptation, the Star, which I had seen at a distance before, began to appear again, and the Day Star arose in my heart.[4] Now did the Spirit of God take possession of my soul, and, as I humbly hope, seal me unto the day of redemption. . . .

---

[1] "Gross and notorious" are active, external sins. "Heart sins" are internal, relating to thoughts or attitudes.
[2] Bishop Joseph Hall, an early-seventeenth-century Anglican devotional writer.
[3] John 19:28. Christ cried out "I thirst" as he was dying on the cross.
[4] 2 Peter 1:19.

Saturday, Feb. 17. Read prayers and expounded the parable of the Prodigal Son[5] at Newgate[6] to a great number of people. . . . About one in the afternoon, I went with my brother Seward,[7] and another friend, to Kingswood, and was most delightfully entertained by an old disciple of the Lord. My bowels[8] have long since yearned toward the poor colliers,[9] who are very numerous, and as sheep having no shepherd. After dinner, therefore, I went upon a mount, and spake to as many people as came unto me. They were upwards of two hundred. Blessed be God that I have now broken the ice! I believe I never was more acceptable to my Master than when I was standing to teach those hearers in the open fields. Some may censure me; but if I thus pleased men, I should not be the servant of Christ. . . .

Monday, May 28. Preached, after earnest and frequent invitation, at Hackney, in a field belonging to one Mr. Rudge, to about ten thousand people. I insisted much upon the reasonableness of the doctrine of the new birth, and the necessity of our receiving the Holy Ghost in His sanctifying gifts and graces, as well now as formerly. God was pleased to impress it most deeply upon the hearers. Great numbers were in tears; and I could not help exposing the impiety of those letter-learned teachers, who say, we are not now to receive the Holy Ghost, and who count the doctrine of the new birth, enthusiasm. Out of your own mouths will I condemn you. Did you not, at the time of ordination, tell the bishop, that you were inwardly moved by the Holy Ghost to take upon you administration of the Church? Surely, at that time you acted the crime of Ananias and Sapphira[10] over again. You lied, not unto man, but unto God. . . .

Friday, June 1. Dined at Old Ford, and gave a short exhortation to a few people in a field, and preached, in the evening, at a place called Mayfair, near Hyde Park Corner. The congregation, I believe, consisted of near eighty thousand people. It was, by far, the largest I ever

---

[5]In Luke 15, Jesus tells the parable of the Prodigal Son, who left his family, squandered his inheritance, and returned home expecting to be shamed. But his father welcomes him back enthusiastically, telling the family that the son who "was lost" is now found.

[6]A prison in London.

[7]William Seward, a wealthy convert who supported and publicized Whitefield's ministry.

[8]Innermost parts.

[9]Coal miners.

[10]Ananias and Sapphira were a husband and wife struck down in Acts 5 for lying about a contribution they made to Christ's apostles.

preached to yet. In the time of my prayer, there was a little noise; but they kept a deep silence during my whole discourse. A high and very commodious scaffold was erected for me to stand upon; and though I was weak in myself, yet God strengthened me to speak so loud, that most could hear, and so powerfully, that most, I believe, could feel. All love, all glory be to God through Christ! . . .

Boston

Friday, September 19. I was visited by several gentlemen and ministers, and went to the Governor's with Esquire Willard, the Secretary of the Province, a man fearing God, and with whom I have corresponded some time, though before unknown in person. The Governor received me with the utmost respect, desired me to see him as often as I could. At eleven, I went to public worship at the Church of England, and afterwards went home with the Commissary,[11] who had read prayers. He received me very courteously; and, it being a day whereon the clergy of the Established Church met, I had an opportunity of conversing with five of them together. I think, one of them began with me for calling "that Tennent and his brethren *faithful* ministers of Jesus Christ." I answered, "I believed they were." They then questioned me about "the validity of the Presbyterian ordination." I replied, "I believed it was valid." They then urged against me a passage in my first *Journal*, where I said, "That a Baptist minister at Deal did not give a satisfactory answer concerning his mission." I answered, "Perhaps my sentiments were altered." "And is Mr. Wesley[12] altered in his sentiments?" said one; "for he was very strenuous for the Church, and rigorous against all other forms of government when he was at Boston." I answered, "He was then a great bigot, but God has since enlarged his heart, and I believed he was now like-minded with me in this particular." I then urged, "That a catholic[13] spirit was best, and that a Baptist minister had communicated lately with me at Savannah." "I suppose," said another, "you would do him as good a turn, and would communicate with him." I answered, "Yes," and urged "that it was best to preach the new birth, and the power of godliness, and not to insist so much on the form: for people would never be brought to one mind as to that; nor did Jesus Christ ever intend it."

---

[11]Timothy Cutler (see Document 2).
[12]John Wesley, founder of the Methodist movement in England.
[13]Interdenominational.

"Yes, but He did," said Dr. Cutler. "How do you prove it?" "Because Christ prayed, 'That all might be one, even as Thou Father and I are One.'" I replied, "That was spoken of the inward union of the souls of believers with Jesus Christ, and not of the outward Church." "That cannot be," said Dr. Cutler, "for how then could it be said, 'that the world might know that Thou hast sent Me?'" He then (taking it for granted that the Church of England was the only true apostolical Church) drew a parallel between the Jewish and our Church, urging how God required all things to be made according to the pattern given in the Mount. I answered, "That before the parallel could be just, it must be proved, that every thing enjoined in our Church was as much of a Divine institution as any rite or ceremony under the Jewish dispensation." I added further, "That I saw regenerate[14] souls among the Baptists, among the Presbyterians, among the Independents, and among the Church folks,—all children of God, and yet all born again in a different way of worship: and who can tell which is the most evangelical?" "What, can you see regeneration with your eyes?" said the Commissary, or words to that effect. . . .

Saturday, September 20. . . .

Preached in the morning to about six thousand hearers, in the Rev. Dr. Sewall's meeting-house; and afterwards, on the common, to about eight thousand; and again, at night, to a thronged company at my lodgings. I spent the remainder of the evening with a few friends, in preparing for the Sabbath. Oh that we may be always in the Spirit on the Lord's Day!

Sunday, September 21. Went in the morning, and heard Dr. Colman preach. Dined with his colleague, the Rev. Mr. Cooper. Preached in the afternoon, to a thronged auditory, at the Rev. Mr. Foxcroft's meeting-house. Immediately after, on the common, to about fifteen thousand; and again, at my lodgings, to a greater company than before. Some afterwards came up into my room; and though hoarse, I was enabled to speak, and could have spoken, I believe, till midnight. To see people ready to hear, makes me forget myself. Oh that it may be my sleep, and my meat and drink to do the will of my Heavenly Father! Oh that all who press to hear the Word, may take the Kingdom of God by force! Amen and Amen.

Monday, September 22. . . .

In the afternoon I went to preach at the Rev. Mr. Checkley's meeting-house; but God was pleased to humble us by a very awful

---

[14]Converted.

providence.[15] The meeting-house being filled, though there was no real danger, on a sudden all the people were in an uproar, and so unaccountably surprised, that some threw themselves out of the windows, others threw themselves out of the gallery, and others trampled upon one another; so that five were actually killed, and others dangerously wounded. I happened to come in the midst of the uproar, and saw two or three lying on the ground in a pitiable condition. God was pleased to give me presence of mind; so that I gave notice I would immediately preach upon the common. The weather was wet, but many thousands followed in the field, to whom I preached from these words, "Go out into the highways and hedges, and compel them to come in."[16] I endeavoured, as God enabled me, to improve[17] what had befallen us. Lord, Thy judgments are like the great deep. Thy footsteps are not known. Just.and Holy art Thou, O King of saints! . . .

Wednesday, September 24. Went this morning to see and preach at Cambridge,[18] the chief college for training the sons of the prophets in New England. It has one president, four tutors, and about a hundred students. The college is scarce as big as one of our least colleges at Oxford; and, as far as I could gather from some who knew the state of it, not far superior to our Universities in piety. Discipline is at a low ebb. Bad books are become fashionable among the tutors and students. Tillotson[19] and Clark[e][20] are read, instead of Shepard,[21] Stoddard,[22] and such-like evangelical writers; and, therefore, I chose to preach from these words, — "We are not as many, who corrupt the Word of God."[23] A great number of neighbouring ministers attended. God gave me great boldness and freedom of speech. The President of the college and minister of the parish treated me very civilly. In the afternoon, I preached again, in the court, when, I believe, there

---

[15]"Providence" is an occurrence sent by God to communicate a specific message.
[16]Luke 14:23.
[17]Take a lesson from.
[18]Harvard College.
[19]John Tillotson, the archbishop of Canterbury in the late seventeenth century, was a popular writer among Anglicans and other English Protestants.
[20]Samuel Clarke, an Anglican priest and philosopher, was accused of Arianism (the belief that God the Father and God the Son are not equal) during his career.
[21]Thomas Shepard was the Puritan pastor in Cambridge, Massachusetts, through the mid-seventeenth century.
[22]Solomon Stoddard, Jonathan Edwards's grandfather.
[23]2 Corinthians 2:17.

were about seven thousand hearers. The Holy Spirit melted many hearts. . . .

Baskinridge[24]

Wednesday, Nov. 5. Set out at eight in the morning, and got to Baskinridge, the place where Mr. Cross exercises his stated ministry, about one o'clock. At the house where I waited in the way, a woman spoke to me under strong convictions, and told me "she was deeply wounded by my last night's discourse." When I came to Baskinridge, I found Mr. [James] Davenport had been preaching to the congregation, according to appointment. It consisted of about three thousand people. I had not discoursed long, when, in every part of the congregation, some one or other began to cry out, and almost all were melted into tears. A little boy, about eight years of age, wept as though his heart would break. Mr. Cross took him up into the waggon, which so affected me, that I broke from my discourse, and told the people that, since old professors were not concerned, God, out of an infant's mouth, was perfecting praise; and the little boy should preach to them. As I was going away, I asked the little boy what he cried for? He answered, his sins. I then asked what he wanted? He answered, Christ. After sermon, Mr. Cross gave notice of an evening lecture in his barn, two miles off. Thither we went, and a great multitude followed. Mr. Gilbert Tennent preached first: and I then began to pray, and gave an exhortation. In about six minutes, one cried out, "He is come, He is come!" and could scarce sustain the manifestation of Jesus to his soul. The eager crying of others, for the like favour, obliged me to stop; and I prayed over them, as I saw their agonies and distress increase. At length we sang a hymn, and then retired to the house, where the man that received Christ continued praising and speaking of Him till near midnight. My own soul was so full that I retired, and wept before the Lord, under a deep sense of my own vileness, and the sovereignty and greatness of God's everlasting love. Most of the people spent the remainder of the night in prayer and praises. It was a night much to be remembered.

[24]Basking Ridge, New Jersey.

4

STEPHEN BORDLEY
On George Whitefield
1739

Stephen Bordley (1710–1764), an Anglican layman in Annapolis, Maryland, heard Whitefield preach in Annapolis in December 1739. Although the lawyer was impressed with the power of Whitefield's oratory, he deplored the emotionalism of the meetings and Whitefield's heightened emphasis on the moving of the Holy Spirit. That emphasis came to distinguish radical evangelicalism, which gave even common people the idea that they could experience God's presence directly. Following is an excerpt from a letter Bordley wrote to his close friend Matthias Harris on December 11, 1739.

Sr. (M. Harris):

I Just now rec[eiv]ed Yours of the 8th Inst[an]t[1] & was in hopes the length of it would have suited that of Your Silence. But I found myself disappointed, and I own it might have given me a good deale of uneasiness, had I not learned from the so much Celebrated Mr. Whit[e]field, that we are entirely to discharge our thoughts of every thing but Jesus and His own Doctrine, and to become fools for Christ's sake. This is perhaps one benefitt I have rec[eiv]ed from two Sermons which that Gent[leman] gave us last friday. And another, and indeed the Chief one is, that by hearing him, I have satisfyed my Curiosity, which otherwise perhaps (from the Great Character which he had, & which came as it were, to prepare the way before him) might have given me a good deale of uneasiness; & that I own is so Compleately satisfyed, that I do not think, had he preached again on Saturday (on which day he left the Town), I should have gone out of doors to have heard him. And now I am giving You a Character of the man from my

---

[1] Of the month.

From Richard J. Cox, ed., "Stephen Bordley, George Whitefield and the Great Awakening in Maryland," *Historical Magazine of the Protestant Episcopal Church*, 46, no. 3 (September 1977): 303–7.

opinion of him, I think myself bound to do it faithfully, & therefore I must declare that I think I never see[n] or heard so fine a delivery as he is master of. His voice is strong and Clear, but not Musical, & he has a little of the West Country twang.[2] He is very Young, has a well turned person, a fine sett of teeth, which is a great ornament in a Speaker & a Sweet and Agreeable turn of Countenance, but the beauty of this is somewhat lessened by a prodigious Squint w[i]th his left Eye. His Acc[ti]on[3] is natural fervent and moving, & the tone and Accent of his Voice together with his Acc[ti]on are so well adapted to each other, that I freely own I never in my life saw any one man that arrived to so great a prefecc[t]ion in the art of Pronunciation as he has done. And indeed it seems to me, to have been his Chief study, for his language is mean & Groveling, without the least Elegance; & his method of discourse is ten times Worse than his language, or rather he has no method at all. His divinity,[4] if he has any, he kept from us, for I heard nothing from him that would even Whisper to me a thought of his having any regular system of it, or of his having ever applyed to any one particular branch of it with a Sufficient attention to make himself master of it. Unless it be the particular of the Holy Spirit, whose Operations are so violent & powerfull in those who are possessed with it, as, according to his Account of it, to enable them to do any thing but work miracles. For in this[,] that is, with regard to the Strength of the Spirit in him, he seems tho' unwillingly, to acknowledge himself to fall short of the Apostles. Tho' soon after he'll rail at all the Clergy in England, & publickly in his Sermons accuse them with what is a most palpable & Impudent lie, & that is, that they all of them preach against the Spirit's being Entertained by us on any account, whereas the Contrary is so notorious that one can hardly look into a printed Sermon, without finding it recommended to us in Express terms, tho' not in so violent a manner as he himself does. This doctrine of the Spirit, & his railing at & accusing the Clergy in the manner before men[ti]on'd, are the great hinges or Supports of all his discourses. For I have heard him preach two, have read one in print, and find them all, tho' on different texts, turn upon the same matters. That in all those Sermons of his which I have heard & read, after the Introduction (wherein they do differ a little from each other)

---

[2]An accent common to the western part of England, where Gloucester, Whitefield's hometown, is.
[3]Preaching style.
[4]Theology.

& before You come near the middle of his discourse, they are alike, almost verbatim to the very end, be the Subjects on which he setts out or his texts, ever so different from each other. From hence You'l[l] easily Judge that he is a very Wretched Divine, & may too in some measure deserve the name, which You or some others bestow on him, of Ranting Enthusiast. . . . There is a Remarkable Circumstance which I had to like have forgot. In all his discourses he very strongly hints, nay sometimes plainly says, that he is divinely Inspired, that he is sent by God on purpose to remove the World from its abominable state of Wickedness, & particularly Where he is railing at the Clergy for preaching (as he says) ag[ains]t the Spirit, he says Yet a little while, & will come the great day of Judgment, And I shall be to Confront You (the Clergy) & to declare what Doctrines You have preached. Oh, it will give me great trouble and uneasiness, but my Duty will oblige me to speak the truth to him Who sent me. And often he tells his Congregation that, he shall be a terrible Witness against them at that Great day, if they do not live up to his foolishness of preaching (as he calls it) & at the same time lays down no rules (at least none predictable) but that of Entertaining the Spirit &c. There is a letter in print said to be wrote by one [William] Seward (one of his followers, of which he has four) to his Brother a Clergyman in Genoa in answer to a letter from him, which seems to me to be Whitefield's own writing, having not only his very language, but is also an Epitome of his Doctrine (which You may read and Edify from if you can) tho' indeed there seems to be a nearer approach to reasoning than I have seen or heard in any of his Sermons. He has putt some among us here on a Wild goose Chase, in quest of that degree of the Spirit Which perhaps they never will find. Others he has thrown into the Vapours & Despair (the Common Effect of his foolishness of preaching in England), & into a full perswasion that the Good man, as he would have them believe, is miraculously Inspired, & 'tis really a difficult matter to perswade some among us here to make a difference between his Doctrine & Delivery. As to the Sanctity of his life, I can say nothing, but that he has that Character, & has lived agreeably to it here. If he is Sincere, he Certainly is a Violent Enthusiast. If not, he is a most Vain & Arrogant Hyprocrite, & I own I should rather Support the latter. He falls Infinitely Short of our favorite pastor's Divinity, tho' he very much Exceeds him in Acc[ti]on & Delivery. In short, he has the best delivery w[i]th the Worst Divinity that I ever mett with.

From y[ou]r very H[um]ble Serv[an]t SB.
Ann[apoli]s.   11. Dec. 1739

5

JOSIAH SMITH

The Character, Preaching, &c. of the Rev. Mr. George Whitefield

1740

Josiah Smith (1704–1781) was the key evangelical pastor in Charleston, South Carolina, during the First Great Awakening, and he became one of Whitefield's foremost proponents. In the widely circulated pamphlet excerpted here, Smith defended Whitefield's teaching and suggested that his appearance might signal the fulfillment of biblical prophecy.

My Design from this Text, is to *shew* my impartial Opinion of that *Son of Thunder*,[1] who has lately grac'd and warm'd *this* Desk; and would have been an Ornament, I think, to the *best* Pulpit in the *Province*. Happy shall I think my self, if I can only clinch the Nails, this great *Master of Assemblies* has already fasten'd....

He renounc'd all Pretensions to the extraordinary Powers & Signs of *Apostleship, Gifts of Healing, Speaking with Tongues, the Faith of Miracles*; Things peculiar to the Ages of Inspiration, and extinct with them. — He also allow'd, these *Feelings* of the Spirit were not in every Person, or at all Times, in the *same Degree*; and that tho' a *full Assurance* were *attainable*, and what every one should labour *to attain*, yet not of absolute *Necessity* to the *Being* of a Christian. — Only he asserted that we *might feel* the Spirit of God, in his *sanctifying* and saving Impressions, and witnessing with our own Spirits. And what is there in all this repugnant to *Reason*! What is there in it, but what is perfectly agreeable to *Scripture*! How can we be *led by the Spirit* or have *Joy in the Holy Ghost*, without some sensible Perceptions of it!...

... He is not *bigotted* to the *Modalities* and lesser *Rites* and *Forms* of Religion, while zealous enough, and very warm and jealous in all its

---

[1] Jesus's disciples James and John are called "sons of thunder" in Mark 3:17.

From Josiah Smith, *The Character, Preaching, &c. of the Rev. Mr. George Whitefield* (Boston, 1740), 1, 9, 15, 19–20.

Essentials, especially in the *divine Honours and Godhead* of his Saviour. He professes Love to *good Men* of *every* Denomination, and told us, that the *Kingdom of Heaven consists not in Meats and Drinks*.[2] He appears to me, a Man full of the *Holy Ghost* and of *Faith*. Tho' his Prayers, in *this* Pulpit, were all *extempore*, yet how *copious*, how *ardent*, with what *Compass* of Thought? . . .

I pretend to no Spirit of *Prophesy*, and can only *conjecture*, and offer the Result of *Observation, Reason*, and the usual *Tendencies* of Things, corroborated by the great Promises, scattered up and down in our Bibles, wherein *glorious Things are spoken of thee, thou City of our God!* The *Prophecies* are usually too dark and *mystic* to be fully understood: The *Seals* of that Book are seldom broken, 'till the several Periods of Accomplishment, which makes *Time* the best and surest Expositor. But certainly, if we can discern the Face of *the Sky* in the Morning, we might make some humble and faint Conjectures at the Times and Seasons, which *the Father* keeps in his own Power. Now we are none of us ignorant, how far the primitive *Spirit* of Christianity has sunk into a mere *Form* of Godliness. Irreligion has been rushing in, even upon the *Protestant World* like a Flood: The dearest and most obvious Doctrines of the *Bible* have fallen into low Contempt; the Principles and Systems of our *good and pious Fathers* have been more and more exploded. And now, behold! God seems to have reviv'd the ancient Spirit and Doctrines. He is raising up of our young Men, with Zeal and Courage, to stem the Torrent. They have been in *Labours more abundant*: They have preach'd with such *Fire, Assiduity* and *Success*; such a solemn Awe have they struck upon their Hearers; so unaccountably have they conquer'd the Prejudices of many Persons; such deep Convictions have their Sermons produced; so much have they rous'd and kindled the Zeal of *Ministers* and *People*; so *intrepidly* do they push thro' all Opposition, that my Soul overflows with Joy, and my Heart is too full to express my *Hopes*. It looks as if some happy Period were opening, to bless the World with *another* Reformation. Some great Things seem to be upon the Anvil, some big Prophesy *at the Birth*; God give it Strength to *bring forth!* May he especially water the good Seed his Servant has so plentifully sown among *us*; may we remember how we have heard, and hold fast; may we cherish Conviction; be fix'd and rooted in our *Christian Faith*; not rebel against the *Light*, nor make Shipwreck at last, by the various Winds of Doctrine which are blowing upon us!

---

[2] External rituals; Hebrews 9:10.

6

BENJAMIN FRANKLIN

Advertisement of Whitefield Engravings

1742

As a young printer and merchant in Philadelphia, Benjamin Franklin (1706–1790) found that among his best-selling items were Whitefield's sermons, journals, and pictures, as shown in this advertisement from the Pennsylvania Gazette.

From *Pennsylvania Gazette*, May 20, 1742.

7

YALE COLLEGE

The Declaration of the Rector and Tutors

1745

Whitefield was all the rage when he first visited New England, as we can see in his Journals *(see Document 3). When he returned in 1745, however, many pastors and educators publicly came out against him for having caused religious divisions and broken up churches. The leaders of Yale College had seen firsthand the effects of radical evangelicalism, which bitterly divided the college in 1741–1742. Whitefield's public suggestions that many of New England's ministers were unconverted threatened to break up not only churches but also the colleges that trained the colonies' ministers. In the* Declaration, *excerpted here, Yale officials partially blamed Whitefield for the radicals' creation of the Shepherd's Tent, an evangelical training academy that operated in nearby New London, Connecticut, during 1742–1743. The Shepherd's Tent drew some students away from Yale.*

It has always appeared to us, that you and other *Itinerants* have laid a *Scheme* to turn the generality of Ministers out of their Places, and to introduce a new Sett of such as should be in a peculiar Manner attached to you; and this you would effect by prejudicing the Minds of People against their Ministers, and thereby induce them to *discard* them or *separate* from them.

And this appe[a]rs to us,

I. Because the Principles which you and the other Itinerants laid down, did naturally and necessarily produce this Effect;—which are these.

1. That *the generality of Ministers are unconverted.* The Scope and Design of a great part of your preaching, when you were in this Coun-

---

From Yale College, *The Declaration of the Rector and Tutors of Yale-College* (Boston, 1745), 4–6, 10–12.

try before, was to represent them as *carnal Pharisees,*[1] and to run a Parallel between them and the Pharisees and false Prophets of old. . . .

2. Another Principle which you have advanced, is, *That all unconverted Ministers are half Beasts and half Devils, and can no more be the Means of any Man's Conversion, than a dead Man can beget a living Child.* . . .

Now from these two Principles, which you have laid down, viz.[2] that the generality of Ministers are unconverted, and that all unconverted Ministers are such *baneful* and *pernicious* Men, it naturally and necessarily follows, that *People ought to discard them, or separate from them.* . . .

. . . It has always appeared to us, that you and other Itinerants have laid a Scheme to vilify and subvert our Colleges, and to introduce a Sett of Ministers into our Churches, by other Ways and Means of Education. . . .

. . . But this is certain, that soon after the Publication of these *Slanders* upon the Colleges, *this* was upon several Accounts in a worse State than it was before. Sundry of the Students ran into Enthusiastic Errors and Disorders, censored and reviled their Governours[3] and others; for which some were expelled, denied their Degrees, or otherwise punished; and some withdrew to that Thing called *the Shepherd's Tent.* And we've been informed, that the Students were told, that there was no Danger in disobeying their present Governours, because there would in a short Time be a great Change in the civil Government, and so in the Governours of the College. All which rendered the Government and Instruction of the College, for a while, far more difficult than it was before.

[1] Jewish religious leaders who opposed Jesus.
[2] Namely.
[3] Superiors.

3

Revivals, Conversions, and Spiritual Experiences

8

GILBERT TENNENT

The Danger of an Unconverted Ministry

1740

Gilbert Tennent (1703–1764), a Presbyterian pastor in New Brunswick, New Jersey, delivered the sermon excerpted here in March 1740 in Nottingham, Pennsylvania. In it, Tennent suggested that a primary cause of lifelessness in churches was that many ministers were unconverted. Revivalists such as Tennent did not count education or religious knowledge as the most important qualification for a minister. An effective minister must have experienced the new birth. If godly Christians received no benefit from a minister's preaching, he argued, they should go elsewhere. In an age of revered pastors, state-supported churches, and strictly maintained parish boundaries (people were generally required to go to the church closest to them), Tennent's sermon had ominous implications for the way many ministers were viewed by the people.

As a faithful Ministry is a great Ornament, Blessing, and Comfort, to the Church of GOD; even the Feet of such Messengers are beautiful:[1]

[1]Isaiah 52:7.

From Gilbert Tennent, *The Danger of an Unconverted Ministry* (Philadelphia, 1740), 3, 7–9, 14, 18–19.

So on the contrary, an ungodly Ministry is a great Curse and Judgment: These Caterpillars labour to devour every green Thing. . . .

1. Natural Men[2] have no Call of GOD to the Ministerial Work, under the Gospel-Dispensation. . . .

2. The Ministry of natural Men is uncomfortable to gracious Souls. . . .

Natural Men, not having true Love to Christ and the Souls of their Fellow-Creatures, hence their Discourses are cold and sapless, and as it were freeze between their Lips! And not being sent of GOD, they want[3] that divine Authority, with which the faithful Ambassadors of Christ are clothed, who herein resemble their blessed Master [Jesus]. . . .

And Pharisee-Teachers, having no Experience of a special Work of the Holy Ghost, upon their own Souls, are therefore neither inclined to, nor fitted for Discoursing, frequently, clearly, and pathetically, upon such important Subjects. The Application of their Discourses, is either short, or indistinct and general. . . .

. . . Pharisee-Teachers will with the utmost Hate oppose the very Work of God's Spirit, upon the Souls of Men; and labour by all Means to blacken it, as well as the Instruments, which the Almighty improves to promote the same; if it comes near their Borders, and interferes with their Credit or Interest. Thus did the Pharisees deal with our Saviour. . . .

4. If the Ministry of natural Men be as it has been represented; Then it is both lawful and expedient to go from them to hear Godly Persons; yes, it's so far from being sinful to do this, that one who lives under a pious Minister of lesser Gifts, after having honestly endeavoured to get Benefit by his Ministry, and yet gets little or none, but does find real Benefit and more Benefit elsewhere; I say, he may lawfully go, and that frequently, where he gets most Good to his precious Soul.

[2]Those who are unconverted.
[3]Lack.

9

NATHAN COLE

A Farmer Hears Whitefield Preach

1740

In 1740, George Whitefield visited Middletown, Connecticut, and turned the world upside down for farmer Nathan Cole (1711–1783). Cole had heard a lot about Whitefield before he came to Middletown, and when he heard that Whitefield was near, he literally dropped his farm implement, grabbed his wife, and galloped to the meeting for fear that they might be too late. Whitefield's preaching convinced Cole that he, too, needed the new birth, and after an awful ordeal, he found salvation. The account excerpted here is a rare and detailed example of a layperson's experience of attending one of Whitefield's meetings. One can see, however, that hearing Whitefield did not immediately precipitate conversion for some. Cole's conversion required his acceptance of the doctrine of "election," the belief that God chose, or elected, only certain people to be saved, based not on their merit but on God's grace.

The Spiritual Travels of Nathan Cole

I was born Feb 15th 1711 and born again octo 1741—

When I was young I had very early Convictions; but after I grew up I was an Arminian untill I was *near* 30 years of age; I intended to be saved by my own works such as prayers and good deeds.

Now it pleased God to send Mr Whitefield into this land; and my hearing of his preaching at Philadelphia, like one of the Old apostles, and many thousands flocking to hear him preach the Gospel; and great numbers were converted to Christ; I felt the Spirit of God drawing me by conviction; I longed to see and hear him, and wished he would come this way. I heard he was come to New York and the

From Michael Crawford, ed., "The Spiritual Travels of Nathan Cole," *William and Mary Quarterly*, 3rd ser., 33, no. 1 (January 1976): 92–94, 96–97.

Jerseys[1] and great multitudes flocking after him under great concern for their Souls which brought on my Concern more and more hoping soon to see him but next I heard he was at long Island; then at Boston and next at Northampton.

Then on a Sudden, in the morning about 8 or 9 of the Clock there came a messenger and said Mr Whit[e]field preached at Hartford and Weathersfield yesterday and is to preach at Middletown this morning[2] at ten of the Clock, I was in my field at Work, I dropt my tool that I had in my hand and ran home to my wife telling her to make ready quickly to go and hear Mr Whit[e]field preach at Middletown, then run to my pasture for my horse with all my might; fearing that I should be too late; having my horse I with my wife soon mounted the horse and went forward as fast as I thought the horse could bear, and when my horse got *much* out of breath I would get down and put my wife on the Saddle and bid her ride as fast as she could and not Stop or Slack for me except I bad her and so I would run untill I was *much* out of breath; and then mount my horse again, and so I did several times to favour my horse; we improved every moment to get along as if we were fleeing for our lives; all the while fearing we should be too late to hear the Sermon, for we had twelve miles to ride double in little more than an hour and we went round by the upper housen parish.[3]

And when we came within about half a mile or a mile of the Road that comes down from Hartford[,] Weathersfield and Stepney to Middletown; on high land I saw before me a Cloud or fogg rising; I first thought it came from the great River,[4] but as I came nearer the Road, I heard a noise something like a low rumbling thunder and presently found it was the noise of Horses feet coming down the Road and this Cloud was a Cloud of dust made by the Horses feet; it arose some Rods into the air over the tops of Hills and trees and when I came within about 20 *rods* of the Road, I could see men and horses Sliping along in the Cloud like shadows and as I drew nearer it seemed like a steady Stream of horses and their riders, scarcely a horse more than his length behind another, all of a Lather and foam with sweat, their breath rolling out of their nostrils every Jump; every horse seemed to go with all his might to carry his rider to hear news from heaven for

[1] New Jersey was split into East and West Jersey until 1702.
[2] Thursday, October 23, 1740.
[3] "Upper housen parish" refers to Middletown Upper Houses Parish, the present town of Cromwell.
[4] Connecticut River.

the saving of Souls, it made me tremble to see the Sight, how the
world was in a Struggle; I found a Vacance between two horses to Slip
in mine and my Wife said law our Cloaths will be all spoiled see how
they look, for they were so Covered with dust, that they looked almost
all of a Color [—] Coats, hats, Shirts, and horses.

We went down in the Stream but heard no man speak a word all the
way for 3 miles but every one pressing forward in great haste and
when we got to Middletown old meeting house there was a great Multitude *it was said to be 3 or 4000* of people Assembled together; we
dismounted and shook of[f] our Dust; and the ministers were then
Coming to the meeting house; I turned and looked towards the Great
River and saw the ferry boats Running swift backward and forward
bringing over loads of people and the Oars Rowed nimble and quick;
every thing—men, horses and boats—seemed to be Struggling for
life; *The land and banks over the river looked black with people and
horses* all along the 12 miles[.] I saw no man at work in his field, but all
seemed to be gone.

When I saw Mr Whit[e]field come upon the Scaffold he Lookt
almost angelical; a young, Slim, slender, youth before some thousands
of people with a bold undaunted Countenance, and my hearing how
God was with him every where as he came along it Solemnized my
mind; and put me into a trembling fear before he began to preach; for
he looked as if he was Cloathed with authority from the Great God;
and a sweet sollome[5] solemnity sat upon his brow[.] And my hearing
him preach, gave me a heart wound; By Gods blessing: my old Foundation was broken up, and I saw that my righteousness would not save
me; then I was convinced of the doctrine of Election: and went right to
quarrelling with God about it; because that all I could do would not
save me; and he had decreed from Eternity who should be saved and
who not.

I began to think I was not Elected, and that God made some for
heaven and me for hell. And I thought God was not Just in so doing, I
thought I did not stand on even Ground with others, if as I thought; I
was made to be damned; My heart then rose against God exceedingly,
for his making me for hell; Now this distress lasted Almost two
years:—Poor—Me—Miserable me.—It pleased God to bring on my
Convictions more and more, and I was loaded with the guilt of Sin, I
saw I was undone for ever; I carried Such a weight of Sin in my breast
or mind, that it seemed to me as if I should sink into the ground every

[5]Solemn.

step; and I kept all to my self as much as I could; I went month after month mourning and begging for mercy, I tryed every way I could think to help my self but all ways failed:—Poor me it took away *most* all my Comfort of eating, drinking, Sleeping, or working. Hell fire was most always in my mind; and I have hundreds of times put my fingers into my pipe when I have been smoaking to feel how fire felt: And to see how my Body could bear to lye in Hell fire for ever and ever. Now my countenance was sad so that others took notice of it. . . .

And there came some body in with a great Arm full of dry wood and laid it on the fire, *and went out* and it burnt up very briskly as I lay on my Bed with my face toward the fire looking on, with these thoughts in my mind, Oh that I might creep into that fire and lye there and burn to death and die for ever Soul and Body; Oh that God would suffer it—Oh that God would suffer it.—Poor Soul.

And while these thoughts were in my mind God appeared unto me and made me Skringe[6]: before whose face the heavens and the earth fled away; and I was Shrinked into nothing; I knew not whether I was in the body or out, I seemed to hang in open Air before God, and he seemed to Speak to me in an angry and Sovereign way what won't you trust your Soul with God; My heart answered O yes, yes, yes; before I could stir my tongue or lips, And then He seemed to speak again, and say, may not God make one Vessel to honour and an other to dishonour and not let you know it;[7] My heart answered again O yes yes before I cou'd stir my tongue or lips. Now while my Soul was viewing God, my fleshly part was working imaginations and saw many things which I will omitt to tell at this time.

When God appeared to me every thing vanished and was gone in the twinkling of an Eye, as quick as A flash of lightning; But when God disappeared or in some measure withdrew, every thing was in its place again and I was on my Bed. My heart was broken; my burden was fallen of[f] my mind; I was set free, my distress was gone, and I was filled with a pineing desire to see Christs own words in the bible; and I got up off my bed being alone; And by the help of Chairs I got along to the window where my bible was and I opened it and the first place I saw was the 15th Chap: John[8]—on Christs own words and they spake to my very heart and every doubt and scruple that rose in my heart about the truth of Gods word was took right off; and I saw

[6]Cringe.
[7]Romans 9:21.
[8]John 15:1: "I am the true vine, and my Father is the husbandman."

the whole train of Scriptures all in a Connection, and I believe I felt just as the Apostles felt the truth of the word when they writ it, every leaf[,][9] line and letter smiled in my face; I got the bible up under my Chin and hugged it; it was sweet and lovely; the word was nigh me in my hand, then I began to pray and to praise God.

I could say Oh my God, and then I could think of no expression good enough to speak to Him, *he was altogether—lovely* and then I wou'd fall down into a muse and look back into my past life to see how I had lived and it seemed as if my very heart strings would break with sorrow and grief, to see how I had lived in abuse to this God I saw; then I began to pray and to praise God again, and I could say Oh my God and then I could not find words good enough to speak to his praise; then I fell into a muse and look'd back on my past life; and saw what an abominable unbeliever I had been, O now I could weep for joy and Sorrow, now I had true mourning for sin and never before now I saw sin to be right against God; now my heart and Soul were filled as full as they Could hold with Joy and sorrow; now I perfectly felt truth: now my heart talked with God; now every thing praised God; the trees, the stone, the walls of the house and every thing I could set my eyes on, they all praised God.

[9]Page.

10

SAMSON OCCOM

Conversion

1740

Samson Occom (1723–1792), a Mohegan Indian, became the most celebrated Native American pastor and missionary in eighteenth-century America. Occom began to hear reports of the revivals among the English colonists as a teenager in Connecticut and then was converted in 1740, partly through radical itinerant James Davenport's influence. Occom

William DeLoss Love, *Samson Occom and the Christian Indians of New England* (Boston: Pilgrim Press, 1899), 23–24, 34.

went on to become a star pupil at Eleazar Wheelock's Charity School, for which Occom later raised funds in England. After Wheelock moved the school to New Hampshire (where it would be called Dartmouth College), Wheelock and Occom's friendship fell apart, with Occom believing that Wheelock had abandoned Christian education for Native Americans and Wheelock spreading rumors that Occom was a drunk. Following is an excerpt from Samson Occom's diary.

I was Born a Heathen and Brought up in Heathenism till I was between 16 and 17 years of age, at a Place Called Mohegan, in New London, Connecticut in New England. My Parents lived a wandering life as did all the Indians at Mohegan. They Chiefly Depended upon Hunting, Fishing and Fowling for their Living and had no connection with the English, excepting to Traffic with them in their small trifles and they strictly maintained and followed their Heathenish ways, customs and Religion. Neither did we cultivate our Land nor keep any Sort of Creatures, except Dogs which we used in Hunting, and we Dwelt in Wigwams. These are a sort of Tent, covered with Matts made of Flags. And to this Time we were unacquainted with the English Tongue in general, though there were a few who understood a little of it. . . .

When I was 16 years of age, we heard a strange Rumor among the English that there were extraordinary Ministers Preaching from Place to Place and a Strange Concern among the White People. This was in the Spring of the Year. But we saw nothing of these things till Some Time in the Summer, when Some ministers began to visit us and Preach the Word of God; and the Common People also came frequently and exhorted us to the things of God which it pleased the Lord, as I humbly hope, to Bless and accompany with Divine Influences to the Conviction and Saving Conversion of a Number of us, amongst whom I was one that was Impresst with the things we had heard. These Preachers did not only come to us, but we frequently went to their meetings and Churches. After I was convicted I went to all the meetings I could come at, & continued under Trouble of Mind about 6 months, at which time I began to Learn the English Letters, got me a Primer and used to go to my English Neighbours frequently for Assistance in Reading, but went to no School. And when I was 17 years of age I had, as I trust, a Discovery of the way of Salvation through Jesus Christ and was enabled to put my trust in him alone for

Figure 4. Samson Occom, 1768, *by Jonathan Spilsbury.*

Samson Occom became the most influential Native American evangelical preacher of the mid-eighteenth century. He adopted English-style dress and manners after he converted, but he eventually broke off his friendship with his main evangelical patron, Eleazar Wheelock.

Hood Museum of Art, Dartmouth College, Hanover, New Hampshire; gift of Mrs. Robert W. Birch.

Life & Salvation. From this Time the Distress and Burden of my mind was removed, and I found Serenity and Pleasure of Soul in Serving God. By this time I just began to Read in the New Testament without Spelling, and I had a Stronger Desire Still to Learn to read the Word of God, and at the Same Time had an uncommon Pity & Compassion to my Poor Brethren According to the Flesh.[1] I used to wish I was Capable of Instructing my poor Kindred. I used to think if I could once Learn to Read I would Instruct the poor Children in Reading and used frequently to talk with our Indians Concerning Religion. Thus I continued till I was in my 19th year, and by this Time I could Read a little in the Bible.

[1] Other Native Americans.

11

HANNAH HEATON

A Farm Woman's Conversion

1741

Like Nathan Cole (see Document 9), Hannah Heaton (1721–1793) was from a farming family in Connecticut, and George Whitefield was instrumental in her conversion. After attending numerous revival meetings and suffering torments from the devil, Heaton finally received a vision of Jesus and experienced the new birth of salvation. Like Cole's account, this excerpt from Heaton's diary communicates well the emotional turmoil and great relief her conversion brought her.

Now after a while I went over to New Haven [Connecticut] in the fall just before that great work of God began which was in the year 1741. There I heard Mr. [Gilbert] Tennent and Mr. Whitefield preach which

From Barbara E. Lacey, ed., *The World of Hannah Heaton: The Diary of an Eighteenth-Century Connecticut Farm Woman* (DeKalb, Ill.: Northern Illinois University Press, 2003), 6–7, 9–10.

awakened me much. Mr. Whitefield laid down the marks of an unconverted person. Oh strange it was, such preaching as I never heard before. "Don't you," said he, "when you are at the house of God long [that the] service should be over that your minds may be about your worldly concerns and pleasures. Is it not a weariness to you," said he, "if one day's serving God is so wearisome to you? How could you endure to be in heaven in this condition? The first prayer you would make would be that you might go into hell, for that would be more agreeable to your natures." "Oh," thought I, "I have found it a weariness to me many a time over and over again." Then I began to think my nature must be changed but how to attain it I knew not. . . .

I had a strong impression upon my mind to go home, which I did in a few days. As soon as I got into my father's house young people came in and began to talk. Sister Elisabeth began to cry over me because I had no interest in Christ. That I wondered at, but the next morning father examined[1] me and I was forced to tell my experiences as well as I could. He told me when I had done what a dreadful condition I was in. It took hold of my heart. I kept going to the meetings and was more and more concerned. And oh what crying out there was among the people, "what shall I do to be saved?" Now it began to be whispered in my ear, "it is too late, too late, you had better hang your self." And when I saw a convenient place [to hang myself] oh how it would strike me. I was afraid to go alone to pray for fear I should see the devil. Once when I was on the ground away alone at prayer trying to give up all to Christ, in great distress of soul I thought I felt the devil twitch my clothes. I jumped up and ran in, fixed with terror, and oh how did I look at the windows in the night to see if Christ was not coming to judgment. Oh how did I envy toads or any creature that had no souls to perish eternally. Many a time I kneeled down to pray and my mouth was as it were stopped, and I did vent out my anguish with tears and groans and a few broken speeches. Now it cut me to think how I had spent my precious time in vanity and sin against God. My not regarding the Sabbath no more was bitter to me now. I thought sometime I could be willing to burn in the flames of fire if I could be delivered from the anger of God, or appease his wrath that was out against me. . . .

. . . I remember in the lot as I went I saw strawberries and these thoughts passed through my mind. "I may as well go to picking strawberries now as not, it's no matter what I do, it's a gone case with me. I

---

[1]Questioned.

fear I have committed the unpardonable sin and now [am] hardened."
But as I was going home I [re]considered at last. I turned and went to
meeting. Soon after meeting began the power of God came down.
Many were crying out [on] the other side of the room, "what shall I
do to be saved?" I was immediately moved to press through the multitude and went to them. A great melting of soul came upon me. I wept
bitterly and pled hard for mercy, mercy. Now I was brought to view
the justice of God due to me for my sin. It made me tremble, my
knees smote² together, then I thought of Belshazzar³ when he saw the
hand writing against him. It seemed to me I was sinking down into
hell. I thought the floor I stood on gave way, and I was just going, but
then I began to resign,⁴ and as I resigned, my distress began to go off
till I was perfectly easy, quiet, and calm. I could say, "Lord, it is just if I
sink into hell." I felt for a few moments like a creature dead. I was
nothing, I could do nothing, nor I desired nothing. I had not so much
as one desire for mercy left [in] me, but presently I heard one in the
room say "seek and you shall find, come to me all you that are weary
and heavy laden, and I will give you rest."⁵ I began to feel a thirsting
after Christ, and began to beg for mercy, free mercy for Jesus's sake. I
thought I saw Jesus with the eyes of my soul stand[ing] up in heaven.
A lovely god-man with his arms open, ready to receive me, his face
was full of smiles, he looked white and ruddy⁶ and was just such a savior as my soul wanted, every way suitable for me. Oh how it melted
my heart to think he had been willing all this while to save me, but I
was not willing, which I never believed before now. I cried from the
very heart to think what a tender-hearted savior I had been refusing.
How often I turned a deaf ear to his gracious calls and invitations. All
that had kept me from him was my will. Jesus appeared altogether
lovely to me now. My heart went out with love and thankfulness
and admiration. I cried "why me Lord? and leave so many?" Oh what a
fullness was there in Christ for others if they would come and give up
their all to him. I went about the room and invited people to come
to him.

June 20, 1741. About nine o'clock in the evening, in the twentieth
year of my age. I got away to go home from meeting. It was about a

²Knocked.
³The king of Babylon against whom God prophesied with mysterious handwriting on
the palace wall in Daniel 5.
⁴Submit.
⁵Matthew 7:7 and 11:28.
⁶Rosy.

mile but oh me [I] thought the moon and stars seemed as if they praised God with me. It seemed as if I had a new soul & body both. I felt a love to God's children. I thought that night that Jesus was a precious Jesus. It being late our family went to bed but I sat up and walked about the chamber. It seemed as if I could not sleep while the heavens were filled with praises and singing.

12

DANIEL ROGERS

Diary

1741–1742

Daniel Rogers (1707–1785) left his position as a tutor at Harvard College to join George Whitefield's entourage in late 1740. Soon after meeting the evangelist, Rogers experienced the new birth. Then he became a radical itinerant, and he led his most successful revivals in his hometown of Ipswich, Massachusetts. In these unpolished entries from his diary, you can sense the fervent and nearly chaotic scenes at the radicals' revival meetings. Note especially the work of female "exhorters" in these selections. Exhorters were not ordained ministers, but laypeople who publicly addressed congregations from time to time. Moderates and antirevivalists often warned the radicals not to treat exhorters like real ministers.

Dec. 27, *Ipswich*. Lord's Day

EVENING

God was pleased to begin a Revival of his work in this Town in a most Glorious manner at a private meeting of young men where a g[reat] Number of the People of the Town were gathered together.—My [dear] Kinsman [John] Rogers—performed the Exercises[1]—as I'm

[1]Such as prayer and preaching.

From Diary of Daniel Rogers, 1740–1751, New-York Historical Society.

Informed, He felt the Power of God in Prayer—and then [preached] in a lively manner—The Power of God came down—my Brother Nathaniel & I were sent for—when we came found some of the Children of God full of the Holy Ghost. Some of them over come with the Love of [Jesus] even to fainting. One had strength to speak out & aloud the Praise of the Admirable Jesus in a Wonderful manner. Several were struck with deep Conviction & discovered It in a Remarkable manner. . . .

[December] 31
. . . The Spirit of God came down in an Astonishing manner—2 or 3 Screamed out—it Spread like fire—I suppose a Thousand People were present. And that Some Hundred—3 or 4—at least cried. So [great] weep[ing] & Lamentation I never heard before, I extended my voice as much as possible—but c[ould] not be heard half over the House. . . .

1. January
We met again—[Brother] Nath[aniel] Prayed—Mr. Jewet [preached]—The People waited—Br[other] Nath[aniel] Exhorted— in the Begin[ning] there was a Sweet motion of the Spirit upon the Children of God. I Spoke aloud of the admirable Love *of Jesus & etc. This Influence went off—I am afraid the Spirit of God was quenched.* But He graciously returned again—to some of His Children—particularly as a Spirit of Supplication & Intercession & *Prophecy*, by which I here mean a Person Speaking The Truths of the *Word* Or Gospel by the Immediate Help—or Influence of the Spirit of God, *This is my Faith.* This Spirit was Evidently to me in Lucy Smith. W[hich] was for 2 *Hours.* Her Prayer was Answered. . . .

January 4
The People met again ab[out] 6 o'clock we began with Singing—then prayed, and Exhorted—our Lord was [present] to wound and heal— 2 Young men. Viz. Gold & Gains came out of Darkness into marvelous Light [—] Rejoiced together In the Sweet Love of [Christ] [—] young Holiday prayed in an Extraordinary manner—[they] all called upon Sinners to come to [Christ]. Some new converts were wonderfully filled with the Holy Ghost—Hannah Harris—Hannah Bishop. Particularly Mr. Isaiah Appleton's Wife[.]
. . . Sitting by the Fire with Br[other] Nathaniel. It came unexpectedly ere[2] I was aware I felt the Sweet Power of his Love in my Heart,

[2] Before.

constraining me to love Him with all my Heart. . . . The Sweet Comforter poured in Comfort and Joy. *Humble Joy.* I know it was into my *Soul.* I appeared to my self to be the Vilest Sinner. God gave me a Sweet Spirit of Supplication and intercession—Tho' I was not quite full yet [this] is far beyond what I ever Experienced before—this Joy is Humbling and abasing. . . . I Had now assurance—was Strong in Faith, [could] call Christ my beloved, My Sweet Saviour, [could] trust Him for all—was made freely to be do & suffer any Thing for his Sake. . . .

January 11th
A.M. went & visited Mrs. Whipple and found her full of Joy, blessing, and praising God. . . . About 6 o'Clock in the Evening the People met. . . . We Sang and exhorted the people. After [this] Mrs. Whipple Spoke against Pride, Covetousness, Self Righteousness, calling herself Mary Magdalene.[3] About this Time the Spirit of God was wonderfully poured down into many new Converts in Love, Joy, & etc. [They] continued blessing and praising God throughout the Evening.

[3] Mary Magdalene was a follower of Jesus whom he delivered from demon possession.

13

A Vision of Heaven and Hell

1742

Although many moderate evangelicals tried to deny or discourage them, radical laypeople and pastors of the Great Awakening reported dreams and visions as a regular part of their spiritual experiences. Antirevivalists pointed to these sorts of experiences as evidence of the individualistic chaos the revivals bred. The following remarkable testimony by an anonymous uneducated layperson reflects common themes in these visions of heaven, hell, angels, Christ, the devil, and the Book of Life. Although the spelling and punctuation have been modernized, the account remains unrefined and surprisingly mystical.

From Douglas L. Winiarski, ed., "Souls Filled with Ravishing Transport: Heavenly Visions and the Radical Awakening in New England," *William and Mary Quarterly*, 3rd ser., 61, no. 1 (January 2004): 43–46.

March the 12 1742

On Tuesday last I being at a meeting Mr. [Benjamin] Pomeroy[1] preached from the 40th chapter of Isaiah 1 and 2 verses.[2] I found my heart in some measure drawn forth to God. Sermon being over my soul was filled with ravishing transport to that degree it seemed there was nothing but a thin paper wall that separated me from perfect glory. My desires increased and my heart still reaching forth after God, at last I fainted, and the last I can remember I found myself at the bottom of a great mountain which lay in my way to the heavenly Canaan. The mountain appeared so steep and high I despaired of ever getting up myself. While I was musing in a loving posture I looked and saw a dove come down from the mountain and told me he would carry me up. And spreading his wing I thought I got on and he [rose with] me [to the top of] the mountain and set me down on a large plain. And looking forward I saw a place I thought was heaven. Then betaking myself to my journey, I looked on my left hand and saw a wild bull coming roaring at me. I felt myself surprised and expected to be devoured by him. He came within a few feet of me roaring and jumping at me but could not reach me while I was in this doleful condition. I looked and saw an angel coming to me and took me by the hand and led me by the bull to that place I thought was heaven, and coming near I saw the gate standing open. He led me in where I thought I saw God the Father and God the Son seated on a throne of glory and the angels bowing and paying their homage and adoration to them. I standing speechless before them a[nd] not being able to join with them. I thought when I came there I should join with saints and angels in praising God but now I found the place was so holy I felt as though I should have shrunk into nothing before them. Christ then looked on me and asked why I looked so sorrowful. I could not answer one word. Then he, taking up the book, he showed me my name written in letters of blood,[3] and looking on me with a smile he told me I must return again. I told him I chose to stay. He told me, no, you must go back again, and I will give you grace to withstand all temptations you shall meet with and stay a while and then I should come again. I asked how long. He told me that wasn't for me to know.

---

[1]A key evangelical itinerant from Hebron, Connecticut.

[2]Isaiah 40:1–2: "Comfort ye, comfort ye my people, saith your God. Speak ye comfortably to Jerusalem, and cry unto her, that her warfare is accomplished, that her iniquity is pardoned: for she hath received of the LORD's hand double for all her sins."

[3]In the Bible, the Book of Life lists all the names of those people who are truly saved. It is referred to in the books of Philemon and Revelation.

I found myself willing to return if it was for the glory of God. And then the angel led me out from that blessed place and brought me back the same way I came before. And when we came by the bull he looked with vengeance on me and roaring he threw the dirt all around him. Finding myself [in] no way daunted I passed over the plain with my guide till I came to the top of the hill. I being left alone, my thought turning which way I should get down, and looking, I saw the dove spreading his wings. I got on and he brought [me] down to the bottom of the hill, where I saw the mouth of hell open and the damned souls wallowing in the flames, shrieking and howling. I saw one come up out of the flames. Looking on me with vengeance, he told me he would have me. Then I began to fear. I saw him grin and gnash his teeth at me. Then I heard a voice: "Fear thou not, I am with thee; be not dismayed, I am thy God. I will strengthen thee, yes, I will help thee, yes, I will uphold thee by the right hand of my righteousness."[4] This put new strength into me. I told Satan I feared him not. The God of heaven was my God. He roared out at me and plunged himself into the flames among the ghastly crew. Then my senses returned to me, and I found my body all disordered with the cramp.

Sir, I was never learned to write nor spell. [Eleazar Wheelock, the recipient of the account, noted below this line, "Sir it appears without your telling of it."]

[4]Isaiah 40:10.

14

MERCY WHEELER

A Physical Healing

1743

Mercy Wheeler of Plainfield, Connecticut, had been rendered unable to walk by a childhood ailment. She was converted before the First Great Awakening began, but during the excitement of the revivals, she began to wonder whether God might instantly heal her, just as she read Jesus had

From Benjamin Lord, *God Glorified in His Works* (Boston, 1743), 29–37.

done for so many in the Gospels. Her healing showed that the bodily effects of the revivals were not limited to shaking or coma-like trances but also occasionally produced instant physical transformations of the sick. Some skeptics thought that Wheeler's story—just like dreams, trances, and visions—was fanciful and dangerous because it would deceive the gullible into expecting miracles.

Never in all this Course of 16 Years did [Mercy Wheeler] go one Step alone, until that wonderful Event happened. . . .

As the neighbouring *Ministers* had frequently, at her Desire attended religious *Fasts* and *Lectures* at her Father's House; so now, at her Request a *Lecture* was appointed to be there on Wednesday, this 25th of *May*, and the Rev. Mr. *Lord* of *Preston* invited to preach it. On the Saturday Evening before, she had a very painful Sense of her Infirmities, and also an extraordinary Experience of the Power and Sweetness of God's Word; which both supported her under her present Trouble, and also encouraged her Faith in God, and Hope that it might be better with her. Thus, *God strengthened her, with Strength in her Soul*, and so, proportioned the *Strength* to the *Day*. For, in this Time of her great Exercise, with Pain in her disordered Joints, and with Weakness in her vital Parts, the Lord appeared for her in the Use of his Word, as he had been wont to do. And first he set home that Word upon her Heart, *Let Patience have its perfect Work.*[1] The Sight she now had of the Will of God in her Affliction, that all was as God, the wise, the good, and faithful God would have it, together with the View she had of her own Unworthiness of any Favour, greatly promoted her Patience and Submission. Then, came that Direction and Promise to her Mind, in Revelation 2:10.—*Be thou faithful unto Death, and I will give thee a Crown of Life*, which greatly encouraged her to hold out. And then, as if she must have a more abundant Consolation, those Words in John 11:40.—*If thou wouldst believe, thou shouldst see the Glory of God*, were brought home with great Power upon her Soul, which led her to view the Help there was for her in God, in the Way of believing; and from that Time, such was the powerful Impression of that Word, that she could not help thinking that God would some Way or other, glorify himself in her further and remarkable Deliverance. Thus her Mind wrought from Day to Day, 'till she had a strong Perswasion, that she should be healed, and that the Power of God would be seen in it, though she knew not how. . . . All Hopes of healing in the

[1]James 1:4.

ordinary Way, seemed to be cut off, and a *Doctor* just before, upon the View of her disordered Joints, had said, he thought she would always be a *Cripple*: But yet, her Faith was strengthened to that Degree, that it didn't seem to her any Thing the more difficult for God to heal her, because her State was as it was. So far from this, that her Faith seemed to rise the *highest*, when her own difficult State appeared the *plainest*. And, notwithstanding every Discouragement in Nature, she remained perswaded, that God would glorify himself in her healing, and her Thoughts ran much upon its being done on the *Lecture-Day* at Hand. On *the Morning* of that Day, her Faith grew stronger still, and she could not help thinking, that she should see the Glory of God *that Day*; but, this no Way served to supersede or prevent her earnest Prayer to God for healing. For, she felt her Soul let out much in seeking to the Lord Jesus to heal her. And her Faith was more and more strengthened by meditating on the *Miracles* of Christ; especially, on his healing the poor *impotent Man*, that had lain so long at the *Pool*.[2] It seems, it had been the Lord's Manner with her, to encourage, and help along, her Faith and Hope by directing her to the View of his Miracles, wrought upon one and another, wherein, she had often a clear Representation of her impotent Case; and also a Soul-reviving View of the Power of Christ; so she had at this Time, and it didn't seem difficult to her, to think that the Lord could and would help her. With this Faith, she entered the Day; and was *strong in Faith* and disposed to *give Glory to God*: Her Mind in an extraordinary raised Frame; and could scarce keep from expressing it out full. When Mr. *Lord* came to attend the Service appointed, She had a great Desire to tell him what she had lately met with, and what her particular Faith was about her healing; but could not do it. And when she saw how she was restrained from it, it appeared to her, that it was best she should keep her Faith to *herself*, lest by her *publishing* it, there might be an Expectation among the People of something extraordinary, or otherways that Improvement be made of it, which might not be for the Glory of God. . . . He preached from Isaiah 57:15. *I dwell in the high and holy Place, with him also that is of a contrite and humble Spirit, to revive the Spirit of the Humble, and to revive the Heart of the contrite ones.*—After he had given some *Description* of the humble Heart, and had spoke of the gracious Presence of God, promised to such an one, & etc. he proceeded to *examine*, whether thus humbled?—She thought she could answer to his Rules of Trial, and say Amen to them,

[2]John 5:1–9.

and take the Comfort thereof. After he had gone through with his Examination, he said, "The Lord will revive the Hearts of the Humble, and if you are truly humble, God will revive you; depend upon it, he will, and fear not. Yea, if for his Glory, he will revive and bring you out of a Furnace." Which seem'd to sink into her Heart, as if the Lord did indeed set it home by his Spirit: Then by the Power of the Word upon her Soul, she fell a *Trembling*; but this without any *Diffidence*³ and *Terror*; for it was given to her at that Time, to believe that the Lord would revive and help her, and bring her out. This involuntary Shaking now, continued but a few Minutes; and Nothing in her Behaviour was there, to interrupt the religious Exercise of the People. Her Mind and Heart kept up, in a raised Frame; but yet she was composed thro' the whole, and was more and more confirmed in it, That the Lord would show his Glory in helping her. After Service was over, Mr. *Newel* asked her how she was; but she was too much overcome, to tell how. And when she began to speak, it was something abruptly—(somewhat like as the Spouse, when overcome with Discoveries, begins thus—*The Voice of my Beloved*) Plainly showing that her Mind was full of Thought, and that her Ideas crowded so fast to the Door of Outlet, that they could not observe the just Order in their Expression, and Manner of coming forth.

She was now set upon the Bed, something spent and overcome. Mr. *Lord* came, and sat down by her, and discoursed with her a little, but soon perceived her to be too much overcome for any Conversation almost: she expressed a great Desire of submitting to the Will of God; but couldn't help talking about her Healing, and said, she saw that Christ was *willing* to heal her. Upon which, Mr. *Lord* replied, that she should have the Will of Christ concerning her. But by this Time she was so overpowered with the Sense of God (as she expressed it) "That she could hardly speak, and could not tell what to compare herself to, but, *An Atom drowned in the Sea*": So swallowed up was she, with the Thoughts and Sense of God, and every Way surrounded with his Power. And then only observed to Mr. *Lord*, that it seemed to her, as if GOD was with her of a Truth—and so stopped—Upon which he replied, "If so, then you are well of it, and I will leave you for the present," which he thought best; because she was much spent, and he was afraid she would be quite overcome with any more Conversation then. So, he got up & walked away among the People, that were yet tarrying in the House. And no sooner was he gone from her, but it

³Lack of confidence.

turned in her Mind—"The *Lecture* is ended, and the Service *all over*, and I am not healed; what is become of my Faith now? Won't it be with me, as it used to be?" Whereupon a Cloud of great Darkness came over her, for a Minute or two; in which Time, she was led again into her self, to see what a poor unworthy Creature she was, and had some such Thoughts of the Wisdom and Goodness of God's Will, that she felt a Disposition to be as God would have her be. Then those Words were repeated to her,—*If thou wilt believe, thou shalt see the Glory of God.* By which her Darkness was carried clear off, and under the Influence of this Word, NOW, she seemed (as she expressed it) "to be *wholly taken out of her self, into the Hands of God*; and enabled to believe that he could and would heal her." Immediately upon which, she felt a strange irresistible Motion and Shaking, which began first with her Hands; and quickly spreading over her whole Frame; in which Time, she felt a kind of Weight upon her; a sort of racking of her Frame; every Joint as it were, working; and as if she was with Hands squeezed together, in her weak Places. As this Trembling went off, her Pains went with it, and she felt *strong*, especially in the *Seat* of Life,[4] where she had been most remarkably *weak*; and from thence Strength diffused it self all over her animal[5] Frame, into her Hips, Knees, Ankles & etc. She felt strong and well, as if she had no Disease upon her, and was under no Difficulty. And as she had this Sensation of new Strength and Freedom, she felt as if she was a raising up, and must rise; and immediately *rose up* and *walked* away among the People, with evident Sprightliness and Vigour, to the Astonishment of her self and those about her. She went this Time near 16 Feet, crying out, "Bless the Lord Jesus, who has healed me!" but was soon damped with this Thought, that she was only in a *Frenzy*, and *not healed*; and the more so, when Mr. *Lord* (surprised at seeing her to walk thus, whom he had just before left impotent and overcome too, so that she could hardly talk) did observe to her, that she was in a Frenzy, and accordingly took hold of her and led her to the Bed, and bid her sit down; yea, even thrust her down. But she could not be confined there; feeling yet strong and at Liberty, she quickly rose up again, with those Words in her *Mind, I have loved thee with an everlasting Love*,[6] and with the high Praises of God in her *Mouth*.[7] Her Soul being filled with

[4]The heart.
[5]Bodily.
[6]Jeremiah 31:3.
[7]Psalm 149:6.

such Admiration and Love, as she declared was inexpressible. Now she walked several Times across the Room with Strength and Steadiness; which even constrained the People to think and say, Verily, This is the Power of God!

15

SAMUEL BLAIR

A Short and Faithful Narrative

1744

Samuel Blair (1712–1751) was the Presbyterian pastor of New Londonderry, Pennsylvania. This excerpt from his account of the revival at his church in 1740 gives us a view of awakenings among the Scots-Irish Presbyterians of the Middle Colonies. He believed, like many other revivalist pastors, that his church had settled into "dead formality" before 1740, but emotional preaching renewed members' spiritual sensitivity. When the revival began in his congregation, the moderate Blair requested that people remain silent during his preaching so that everyone could hear him: he did not relish noisy meetings the way radicals did. Although his narrative followed the style set by Jonathan Edwards's A Faithful Narrative *(see Document 1), Blair's account stands out for its detailed description of one woman's deeply emotional conversion experience, which forms the second half of this excerpt. After a long struggle, in which her fear of hell temporarily rendered her deaf and blind, she finally broke through to the new birth during the sacrament of Communion, a celebration that was often central to the Scots-Irish revival tradition on both sides of the Atlantic.*

That it may the more clearly appear that the Lord has indeed carried on a Work of true real Religion among us of late Years, I conceive it will be useful to give a brief general View of the State of Religion in

From Samuel Blair, *A Short and Faithful Narrative, of the Late Remarkable Revival of Religion* (Philadelphia, 1744), 7–8, 10–16, 28–36.

these Parts before this remarkable Season. I doubt not then, but there were still some sincerely religious People up and down; and there were, I believe, a considerable Number in the several Congregations pretty exact, according to their Education, in the Observance of the external Forms of Religion, not only as to Attendance upon publick Ordinances on the Sabbaths, but also, as the Practice of Family Worship, and perhaps secret Prayer too; but, with these Things the most Part seemed to all Appearance to rest contented; and to satisfy their Consciences just with a dead Formality in Religion. . . . The Nature and Necessity of the *New-Birth* was but little known or thought of, the Necessity of a Conviction of Sin and Misery, by the Holy Spirits opening and applying the Law to the Conscience, in order to [attain] a saving Closure with Christ was hardly known at all to the most. . . .

Thus Religion lay as it were a dying, and ready to expire its last Breath of Life in this Part of the visible Church: And it was in the Spring *Anno Domini* 1740, when the God of Salvation was pleased to visit us with the blessed Effusions of his Holy Spirit in an eminent Manner. The first very open and Publick Appearance of this gracious Visitations in these Parts, was in the Congregation which God has committed to my Charge. The Congregation has not been erected above Fourteen or Fifteen Years from this Time: The Place is a new Settlement, generally settled with People from Ireland. (As all our Congregations in *Pennsylvania*, except two or three, chiefly are made up of People from that Kingdom) I am the first Minister they have ever had settled in the Place. . . . In the beginning of *March* I took a Journey into *East-Jersey*, and was abroad for two or three Sabbaths. A neighbouring Minister, who seemed to be earnest for the Awakening and Conversion of secure Sinners, and whom I had obtained to preach a Sabbath to my Peo[ple] in my Absence, preached to them, I think, on the first Sabbath after I left Home. His Subject was the dangerous and awful Case of such as continue unregenerate and unfruitful under the Means of Grace. The Text was *Luke* 13:7. *Then said he to the Dresser of his Vineyard, behold, these three Years I come seeking Fruit on this Fig Tree, and find none, cut it down, why cumbereth it the Ground?* Under that Sermon there was a visible Appearance of much Soul-Concern among the Hearers, so that some burst out with an audible Noise into bitter crying (a Thing not known in those Parts before). . . .

The News of this very publick Appearance of deep Soul-concern among my People met me an Hundred Miles from Home: I was very joyful to hear of it, in Hopes that God was about to carry on an extensive Work of converting Grace amongst them And the first Sermon I preached after my Return to them, was from Mattthew 6:33. *Seek ye first the Kingdom of God, and his Righteousness.* After opening up and explaining the Parts of the Text, when in the Improvement, I came to press the Injunction in the Text upon the Unconverted and Ungodly, and offered this as one Reason among others, why they should now henceforth first of all *seek the Kingdom and Righteousness of God,* viz. That they had neglected too long to do so already. This Consideration seemed to come and cut like a Sword upon several in the Congregation, so that while I was speaking upon it they could no longer contain, but burst out in the most bitter Mourning. I desired[1] them, as much as possible, to restrain themselves from making a Noise that would hinder themselves or others from hearing what was spoken: And often afterwards I had Occasion to repeat the same Council. I still advised People to endeavour to moderate and bound their Passions, but not so as to resist or stifle their Convictions. The Number of the Awakened increased very fast, frequently under Sermons there were some newly convicted, and brought into deep Distress of Soul about their perishing Estate. Our Sabbath Assemblies soon became vastly large; many People from almost all Parts around inclining very much to come where there was such Appearance of the divine Power and Presence. I think there was scarcely a Sermon or Lecture preached there through that whole Summer, but there were manifest Evidences of Impressions on the Hearers; and many Times the Impressions were very great and general: Several would be overcome and fainting; others deeply sobbing, hardly able to contain, others crying in a most dolorous Manner, many others more silently Weeping and a solemn Concern appearing in the Countenance of many others. And sometimes the Soul Exercises of some (though comparatively but very few) would so far affect their Bodies, as to Occasion some strange unusual Bodily Motions. . . .

. . . I have more lately noted down an Account of some of the Soul-Exercises and Experiences of one Person, which I think may be proper to make Publick on this Occasion. The Person is a single Young Woman, but I judge it proper to conceal her Name, because she is yet living. . . .

When she saw People in deep Distress about their Souls' States, she thought with her self how unconcerned she was about her own.

---

[1]Asked.

And though she thought that she had not been very guilty of great Sins yet she feared that she was too little concerned about her eternal well Being. . . . And thus it fared with her, till one Day as she was hearing a Sermon preached from *Hebrews* 3:15. *Today if you will hear his Voice, harden not your Hearts.* The Minister in the Sermon spoke to this Effect. "How many of you have been hearing the Gospel for a long Time, and yet your Hearts remain always hard without being made better by it: The Gospel is the Voice of God, but you have heard it only as the Voice of Man and not the Voice of God, and so have not been benefited by it." These Words came with Power to her Heart: She saw that this was her very Case indeed, and she had an awful Sense of the Sin of her Misimprovement of the Gospel, of her Stupidity, Hardness and Unprofitableness under hearing of the Word of God: She saw that she was hereby exposed to the Sin-punishing Justice of God, and so was fill'd with very great Fear and Terror; but she said there was no other Sin at that Time applied to her Conscience, neither did she see her self as altogether without CHRIST. This deep Concern on the forementioned Account stuck pretty close by her afterward. There was a Society of private Christians to meet in the Neighbourhood some Day after in the same Week for Reading, Prayer and religious Conference, she had not been at a Society of that kind before, but she long'd very much for the Time of their Meeting that she might go there; and while she was there, she got an awful View of her Sin and Corruption, and saw that she was without CHRIST and without Grace, and her Exercise and Distress of Soul was such, that it made her for a while both deaf and blind. . . . She continued for some Weeks in great Distress of Spirit, seeing and pleading for Mercy without any Comfort, until one Sabbath Evening, in a House where she was lodged during the Time of a sacramental Solemnity,[2] while the Family were singing the 84th Psalm, her Soul conceived strong Hopes of Reconciliation with God through JESUS CHRIST, and she had such Apprehensions of the Happiness of the Heavenly State that her Heart was filled with Joy unspeakable and full of Glory, she sung with such Elevation of Soul as if she had sung out of her self, as she expressed it; she thought at the Time it was as if the Lord had put by the Veil and showed her the open Glory of Heaven. She had very enlarged Views of the Sufficiency of CHRIST to save. She was clearly perswaded to the fullest Satisfaction that there was Merrit enough in him to answer for the Sins of the

---

[2]The traditional Scots-Irish Communion festival.

most guilty Sinner, and she saw that God could well be reconciled to all elect Sinners in his Son, which was a most ravishing delightful Scene of Contemplation to her. . . . After she had been so long under an almost alternate Succession of Troubles and Supports, the Sun of Righteousness at last broke out upon her to the clear Satisfaction and unspeakable Ravishment of her Soul at a Communion Table, there her Mind was let into the glorious Mysteries of Redemption, with great Enlargement while she meditated on the Sufferings of the Lord Jesus, she thought with her self, he was not just a Man who suffered so for Sinners; but infinitely more than a Man, even the most High God, the eternal Son equal with the Father, and she saw that his being God, put an infinite Luster and Value upon his Sufferings as Man. Her Heart was filled with a most unutterable Admiration of his Person, his Merit and his Love, she was enabled to believe in him with a strong self-evidencing Faith, she believed that he suffered for her Sins, that she was the very Person, who by her Sins had occasioned his Sufferings, and brought Agony and Pain upon him. The Consideration of this filled her with the deepest Abhorrence of her Sins, and most bitter Grief for them, she said she could have desired with all her Heart to have melted and dissolved her Body quite away in that very Place, in Lamentation and Mourning over her Sins. After this Enjoyment her Soul was generally delighting in God, and she had much of the Light of his Countenance with her, and Oh! her great Concern still was how she might live to the Lord, how she might do any Thing for him, and give Honour to him. The Lord condescended to be much with her by his enlivening and comforting Presence, and especially sacramental Seasons were blessed and precious Seasons to her. . . . The Glory and Delight let in upon her Soul . . . was so great that it quite overcome her bodily Frame, she said it seemed to her that she was almost all Spirit, and that the Body was quite laid by, and she was sometimes in Hopes that the Union would actually break, and the Soul get quite away.

16

SAMUEL BUELL

A Faithful Narrative
of the Remarkable Revival of Religion

1766

Samuel Buell was a young Yale graduate in the early 1740s when he became one of the most electrifying itinerants of the early revivals. Later, he became a pastor in Easthampton, Long Island (New York), but he never gave up hope for more revivals like those of the 1740s. In 1764, Buell saw a major revival break out in his congregation, and word of the revival spread and inspired other awakenings across Long Island and in New England. This excerpt picks up just as the most fervent part of the revival began. Written self-consciously in the style of his mentor Jonathan Edwards, Buell's A Faithful Narrative of the Remarkable Revival of Religion *(1766) gave a vivid account of the intense emotions on display, which Buell likened to scenes of Christ's Second Coming. Buell's account helps demonstrate that although the period 1740 to 1743 saw the height of the Great Awakening, local revivals continued to occur, sometimes led by the same people who spurred the excitement of the early 1740s.*

About 2 o'clock we all met in solemn Assembly.... There was much Solemnity and Seriousness upon the Face of the Assembly; yet the People seemed to be waiting for an increasing Sense of divine Things.... I repeatedly charged the People in the most solemn Manner, and beseeched them again and again, to give God the Glory, all the Glory, if He should now condescend to grant a marvelous Outpouring of the Spirit. Immediately thereupon as I proceeded to Speak, there appeared to be a most surprising Effusion of the Holy Spirit, upon People in all parts of the House....

... The Report of what God was doing among us, had now spread abroad, and many People from neighboring Congregations came to

---

From Samuel Buell, *A Faithful Narrative of the Remarkable Revival of Religion* (New York, 1766), 11–17.

join with us in the solemn Services of this Day. So that we had now
the largest Assembly I ever saw upon this End of our Isle. . . .

From Day to Day, I now saw many Sinners of various Ages, upon
their Knees, with Hands extended toward Heaven, and in flowing
Tears, begging and crying for the Exercise of sovereign Mercy in the
name of Jesus, with as much Earnestness and Importunity, to all
Appearance, as though the Lord Jesus Christ was then coming in flaming Fire to the final Judgment. They seem'd to be pressing into the
Kingdom of God, as if they would take it by Violence.[1] . . .

. . . Some of them especially appeared like primitive[2] Christians full
of the Holy Ghost, rejoicing in the Lord. While the Comforts of Some,
and the Distress of Others, ran so high and became so great, as set in
Contrast and standing opposed, we had, as it were, a Sort of Resem-
blance of the Day of final Judgment, and it appeared as if Persons
were now entering upon their eternal States of Heaven and Hell. It is
indeed beyond me to give a full Description of this wonderful Scene.

[1]Matthew 11:12.
[2]Original or ancient.

17

JOHN MARRANT

A Narrative of the Lord's Wonderful Dealings

1785

*John Marrant (1755–1791) was born a free African American in New
York but moved with his family to South Carolina, where he became a
tradesman's apprentice and an aspiring musician. In 1770, he and a
friend encountered a revival meeting in Charleston led by George Whitefield. Marrant's dramatic conversion and forced service in the British
navy led eventually to his ordination in England into the Countess of*

From John Marrant, *A Narrative of the Lord's Wonderful Dealings with John Marrant*
(London, 1785), in *"Face Zion Forward": First Writers of the Black Atlantic, 1785–1798*,
ed. Joanna Brooks and John Saillant (Boston: Northeastern University Press, 2002),
49–53.

Huntingdon's Connexion, a Calvinistic sect of Methodists. In 1785, Mar-rant returned to North America to serve as a minister in Nova Scotia's large community of Loyalist blacks displaced by the American Revolu-tion. In this excerpt, the young, flippant Marrant goes into Whitefield's meeting planning to disrupt it. But when Whitefield seems to speak directly to him, Marrant is briefly knocked unconscious. Soon Marrant breaks through to his conversion.

I, John Marrant, born June 15th, 1755, in New-York, in North-America, wish these gracious dealings of the Lord with me to be published, in hopes they may be useful to others, to encourage the fearful, to con-firm the wavering, and to refresh the hearts of true believers. My father died when I was little more than four years of age, and before I was five my mother removed from New-York to St. Augustine [Florida], about seven hundred miles from that city. Here I was sent to school, and taught to read and spell; after we had resided here about eighteen months, it was found necessary to remove to Georgia, where we remained; and I was kept to school until I had attained my eleventh year. The Lord spoke to me in my early days, by these removes, if I could have understood him, and said, "Here we have no continuing city." We left Georgia, and went to Charles-Town,[1] where it was intended I should be put apprentice to some trade. Some time after I had been in Charles-Town, as I was walking one day, I passed by a school, and heard music and dancing, which took my fancy very much, and I felt a strong inclination to learn the music. . . . My improvement was so rapid, that in a twelve-month's time I became master both of the violin and of the French-horn, and was much respected by the Gentlemen and Ladies whose children attended the school, as also by my [school]master. This opened to me a large door of vanity and vice, for I was invited to all the balls and assemblies that were held in the town, and met with the general applause of the inhab-itants. I was a stranger to want, being supplied with as much money as I had any occasion for; which my sister observing, said, "You have now no need of a trade." I was now in my thirteenth year, devoted to pleasure and drinking in iniquity like water; a slave to every vice suited to my nature and to my years. The time I had engaged to serve my master being expired, he persuaded me to stay with him, and offered me any thing or any money, not to leave him. His intreaties

[1] Charleston.

proving ineffectual, I quitted his service, and visited my mother in the country; with her I staid two months, living without God or hope in the world, fishing and hunting on the sabbath-day. Unstable as water, I returned to town, and wished to go to some trade. My sister's husband being informed of my inclination provided me with a master, who was a carpenter in that town, on condition that I should serve him one year and a half on trial, and afterwards be bound,[2] if he approved of me. Accordingly I went, but every evening I was sent for to play on music, somewhere or another; and I often continued out very late, sometimes all night, so as to render me incapable of attending my master's business the next day; yet in this manner I served him a year and four months, and was much approved of by him. He wrote a letter to my mother to come and have me bound, and whilst my mother was weighing the matter in her own mind, the gracious purposes of God, respecting a perishing sinner, were now to be disclosed. One evening I was sent for in a very particular manner to go and play for some Gentlemen, which I agreed to do, and was on my way to fulfil my promise; and passing by a large meeting house I saw many lights in it, and crowds of people going in. I enquired what it meant, and was answered by my companion that a crazy man was hallooing there; this raised my curiosity to go in, that I might hear what he was hallooing about. He persuaded me not to go in, but in vain. He then said, "If you will do one thing I will go in with you." I asked him what that was? He replied, "Blow the French-horn among them." I liked the proposal well enough, but expressed my fears of being beaten for disturbing them; but upon his promising to stand by and defend me, I agreed. So we went, and with much difficulty got within the doors. I was pushing the people to make room, to get the horn off my shoulder to blow it, just as Mr. Whitefield was naming his text, and looking round, as I thought, directly upon me, and pointing with his finger, he uttered these words, "PREPARE TO MEET THY GOD, O ISRAEL."[3] The Lord accompanied the word with such power, that I was struck to the ground, and lay both speechless and senseless near half an hour. When I was come a little to, I found two men attending me, and a woman throwing water in my face, and holding a smelling bottle to my nose; and when something more recovered, every word I heard from the minister was like a parcel of swords thrust in to me, and what added to my distress, I thought I saw the devil on every side of me. I was constrained in the

[2]Temporarily indentured as an apprentice.
[3]Amos 4:12.

bitterness of my spirit to halloo out in the midst of the congregation, which disturbing them, they took me away; but finding I could neither walk or stand, they carried me as far as the vestry,[4] and there I remained till the service was over. When the people were dismissed Mr. Whitefield came into the vestry, and being told of my condition he came immediately, and the first word he said to me was, "JESUS CHRIST HAS GOT THEE AT LAST." . . . In this distress of soul I continued for three days without any food, only a little water now and then. On the fourth day, the minister Mr. Whitefield had desired to visit me came to see me, and being directed up-stairs, when he entered the room, I thought he made my distress much worse. He wanted to take hold of my hand, but I durst not give it to him. He insisted upon taking hold of it, and I then got away from him on the side of the bed; but being very weak I fell down, and before I could recover he came to me and took me by the hand, and lifted me up, and after a few words desired to go to prayer. So he fell upon his knees, and pulled me down also; after he had spent some time in prayer he rose up, and asked me how I did now; I answered, much worse; he then said, "Come, we will have the old thing over again," and so we kneeled down a second time, and after he had prayed earnestly we got up, and he said again, "How do you do now"; I replied worse and worse, and asked him if he intended to kill me? "No, no," said he, "You are worth a thousand dead men, let us try the old thing over again," and so falling upon our knees, he continued in prayer a considerable time, and near the close of his prayer, the Lord was pleased to set my soul at perfect liberty, and being filled with joy I began to praise the Lord immediately; my sorrows were turned into peace, and joy, and love. The minister said, "How is it now?" I answered, all is well, all happy.

[4]A room adjacent to the sanctuary.

4

Defining the Boundaries
of the Great Awakening

18

JONATHAN EDWARDS

The Distinguishing Marks
1741

Jonathan Edwards used his Yale commencement address in 1741 to offer a major defense of the awakenings. In this excerpt, Edwards cleverly explains that the Great Awakening could not be judged by its momentary excesses, but only by its long-term results. By these standards, Edwards judged the revivals to be, on the whole, a great work of God. Although he would later become more moderate, as of 1741 Edwards remained very tolerant of the radical camp's excesses.

My design therefore at this time is to shew what are the true, certain, and distinguishing evidences of a work of the Spirit of God, by which we may proceed safely in judging of any operation we find in ourselves, or see in others. . . .

. . . I would prepare my way by first observing negatively, in some instances, what are not signs that we are to judge of a work by, whether it be the work of the Spirit of God or no; and especially, what

From Jonathan Edwards, *The Distinguishing Marks of a Work of the Spirit of God*, in *The Great Awakening*, vol. 4, *The Works of Jonathan Edwards*, ed. C. C. Goen (New Haven, Conn.: Yale University Press, 1972), 227–28, 230, 234–35, 238, 241, 243–44, 246–51, 253, 255, 260–64, 275–76.

are no evidences that a work that is wrought amongst a people, is not the work of the Spirit of God.

1. Nothing can certainly be concluded from this, that the work that appears is carried on in a way very unusual and extraordinary. . . .

2. A work is not to be judged of by any effects on the bodies of men; such as tears, trembling, groans, loud outcries, agonies of body, or the failing of bodily strength. . . .

3. 'Tis no argument that an operation that appears on the minds of a people, is not the work of the Spirit of God, that it occasions a great ado, and a great deal of noise about religion. . . .

4. 'Tis no argument that an operation that appears on the minds of a people, is not the work of the Spirit of God, that many that are the subjects of it, have great impressions on their imaginations. . . .

5. 'Tis no sign that a work that appears, and is wrought on the minds of people, is not from the Spirit of God, that example is made use of as a great means of it. . . .

6. 'Tis no sign that a work that is wrought amongst a people is not from the Spirit of God, that many that seem to be the subjects of it are guilty of great imprudences and irregularities in their conduct. . . .

7. Nor are many errors in judgment, and some delusions of Satan intermixed with the work, any argument that the work in general is not the work of the Spirit of God. . . .

8. If some such as were thought to be wrought upon, fall away into gross errors or scandalous practices, 'tis no argument that the work in general is not the work of the Spirit of God. . . .

9. 'Tis no argument that a work is not from the Spirit of God, that it seems to be promoted by ministers insisting very much on the terrors and that with a great deal of pathos and earnestness. If there be really a hell of such dreadful, and never-ending torments, as is generally supposed, that multitudes are in great danger of, and that the bigger part of men in Christian countries do actually from generation to generation fall into, for want of a sense of the terribleness of it, and their danger of it, and so for want of taking due care to avoid it; then why is it not proper for those that have the care of souls, to take great pains to make men sensible of it? Why should not they be told as much of the truth as can be? If I am in danger of going to hell, I should be glad to know as much as possibly I can of the dreadfulness of it. . . .

Having thus shown, in some instance, what are not evidences that a work that is wrought among a people is not a work of the Spirit of

God, I now proceed in the second place, as was proposed, to shew positively, what are the sure, distinguishing, Scripture evidences and marks of a work of the Spirit of God, by which we may proceed in judging of any operation we find in ourselves, or see among a people, without danger of being misled. . . .

1. When that spirit that is at work amongst a people is observed to operate after such a manner, as to raise their esteem of that Jesus that was born of the Virgin, and was crucified without the gates of Jerusalem; and seems more to confirm and establish their minds in the truth of what the Gospel declares to us of his being the Son of God, and the Saviour of men; 'tis a sure sign that that spirit is the Spirit of God. . . .

2. When the spirit that is at work operates against the interest of Satan's kingdom, which lies in encouraging and establishing sin, and cherishing men's worldly lusts; this is a sure sign that 'tis a true, and not a false spirit. . . .

3. That spirit that operates in such a manner, as to cause in men a greater regard to the Holy Scriptures, and establishes them more in their truth and divinity, is certainly the Spirit of God. . . .

5. If the spirit that is at work among a people operates as a spirit of love to God and man, 'tis a sure sign that 'tis the Spirit of God. . . .

. . . From what has been said, I will venture to draw this inference, viz. that that extraordinary influence that has lately appeared on the minds of the people abroad in this land, causing in them an uncommon concern and engagedness of mind about the things of religion, is undoubtedly, in the general, from the Spirit of God. . . .

As to this work that has lately been carried on in the land, there are many things concerning it that are notorious, and known by everybody (unless it be some that have been very much out of the way of observing and hearing indeed) that unless the Apostle John was out in his rules, are sufficient to determine it to be in general, the work of God. 'Tis notorious that the spirit that is at work, takes off persons' minds from the vanities of the world, and engages them in a deep concern about a future and eternal happiness in another world, and puts them upon earnestly seeking their salvation, and convinces them of the dreadfulness of sin, and of their own guilty and miserable state as they are by nature. It is notorious that it awakens men's consciences, and makes 'em sensible of the dreadfulness of God's anger, and causes in them a great desire, and earnest care and endeavor to obtain his favor. It is notorious that it puts them upon a more diligent improvement of the means of grace which God has appointed. It is also notorious that, in general, it works in persons a greater regard to the Word of God, and desire of hearing and reading of it, and to be more conversant with the Holy Scriptures than they used to be. And it is notoriously manifest that the spirit that is at work, in general, operates as a spirit of truth, making persons more sensible of what is really true, in those things that concern their eternal salvation: as that they must die, and that life is very short and uncertain; that there is a great, sin-hating God that they are accountable to, and will fix them in an eternal state in another world; and that they stand in great need of a Saviour. It is furthermore notorious that the Spirit that is at work makes persons more sensible of the value of that Jesus that was crucified, and their need of him; and that it puts them upon earnestly seeking an interest in him. It can't be but that these things should be apparent to people in general through the land: for these things ben't[1] done in a corner; the work that has been wrought has not been confined to a few towns, in some remoter parts of the land, but has been carried on in many places in all parts of the land, and in most of the principal, and most populous, and public places in it (Christ in this respect has wrought amongst us, in the same manner that he wrought his miracles in Judea), and has now been continued for a considerable time; so that there has been a great deal of opportunity to observe the manner of the work. And all such as have been much in the way of observing the work, and have been very conversant with those that have been the subjects of it, do see a great deal more that, by the rules of the Apostle, does clearly and certainly shew it to be the work of God. . . .

And as I am one that, by the providence of God, have for some months past, been much amongst those that have been the subjects of that work that has of late been carried on in the land; and particularly, have been abundantly in the way of seeing and observing those extraordinary things that many persons have been much stumbled at; such as persons crying out aloud, shrieking, being put into great agonies of body, and deprived of their bodily strength, and the like, and that in many different towns; and have been very particularly conversant with great numbers of such, both in the time of their being subjects of such extraordinary influences and afterwards, from time to time, and have seen the manner and issue of such operations and the fruits of them, for several months together; many of them being per-

---

[1] Be not.

sons that I have long known, and have been intimately acquainted with them in soul concerns, before and since: so I look upon myself called on this occasion to give my testimony, that so far as the nature and tendency of such a work is capable of falling under the observation of a bystander, to whom those that have been the subjects of it have endeavored to open their hearts, or can be come at by diligent and particular inquiry, this work has all those marks that have been spoken of; in very many instances, in every article; and particularly in many of those that have been the subjects of such extraordinary operations, all those marks have appeared in a very great degree. . . .

If there are any that will still resolutely go on to speak contemptibly of these things, I would beg of them to take heed that they ben't guilty of the unpardonable sin[2] against the Holy Ghost.[3] A time when the Holy Spirit is much poured out, and men's lusts, lukewarmness and hypocrisy reproached by its powerful operations, is the most likely time of any whatsoever, for this sin to be committed. If the work goes on, 'tis well if among the many that shew an enmity against it, and reproach it, some ben't guilty of this sin, if none have been already. Those that maliciously oppose and reproach this work, and call it the work of the Devil, want but one thing of the unpardonable sin, and that is doing it against inward conviction. . . .

. . . I come now in the third and last place, to apply myself to those that are the friends of this work, and have been partakers of it, and are zealous to promote it. Let me earnestly exhort such to give diligent heed to themselves to avoid all errors and misconduct, and whatsoever may darken and obscure the work, and give occasion to those that stand ready to reproach it.

[2]Matthew 12:31.
[3]"Holy Ghost," "Holy Spirit," and "Spirit of God" are interchangeable terms.

19

A.M.

The State of Religion in New England

1742

The antirevivalist author of this piece, likely Boston minister Charles Chauncy (1705–1787), sought to paint the revivals in New England as pure chaos, breeding disorder and godlessness. He is particularly harsh in his assessment of George Whitefield, Gilbert Tennent (spelled Tennant here), and James Davenport. The pamphlet was published in Glasgow, where many interested observers wondered how to assess the surprising news coming from America.

May 24, 1742

Sir:

I am sorry you have had such Accounts of Persons and Things transmitted to you from this Country, as you mention in your Letter. They are far from being true, and must come from Men of narrow Minds and great Bigottry, or such as basely affect Popularity, or well-meaning but weak Christians, of little knowledge of Human Nature, or the History of Mankind. Indeed some Persons of very good Sense were once inclined to think that God was doing Wonders in this Place. But that was at a Time when the superstitious Pannick run very high, and bore down everybody that was not well fixed and established either by a natural Steadiness of Temper, or by strong Reason and Reflection. But as soon as the Passions of the People subsided, and Men could coolly and calmly consider, almost every one of but tolerable Sense and Understanding in religious Matters, in great measure changed their Opinions of the Spirit that prevailed here, and had been raised by *Whitefield* and *Tennant.*

The first mentioned of these Gentlemen collected in this Province between five and six hundred Pounds *Sterling* for his *Orphan-house* in *Georgia.* He was a bold and importunate Beggar; he took all Ways

From A.M., *The State of Religion in New England* (Glasgow, 1742), 3–14.

imaginable to persuade the People to give him Money; and he was insatiable as the Grave. . . .

   Mr. *Tennant* in a few Months after Mr. *Whitefield* was gone, came to carry on the Work which he had begun. For several Years, this Man hath been a settled Minister in the *Jerseys*, a Colony about three hundred Miles South-west from *Boston*; and as I have often heard, he hath always been remarkable in those Parts for his uncharitable and divisive Courses. He is a Man of but poor natural Parts, and no Learning, except a little in the disputed Points between the *Calvinists* and *Arminians*. In the Pulpit he was when he first came here, an awkward and ridiculous Ape[1] of *Whitefield*, for his Appearance is very clownish. His great Business in his Sermons was either to puzzle or to frighten his Hearers, but especially the last, which he did by roaring out and bellowing, *Hell, Damnation, Devils*, and all the *Dreadful Words* he could think of. Ministers in general he called Carnal, Unconverted, Blind-leaders-of-the-blind, rational, moral, dry, husky Preachers, that were leading their People to Hell. He exhorted the People to leave them, to go about exhorting one another, and telling their Experiences. He was followed by all sorts of People, as much as *Whitefield* was, and by many preferr'd to him. He was most censorious and uncharitable. Every one that was not exactly of his Mind, he damned without Mercy. His Sermons sometimes were as confused and senseless as you can imagine. He seemed to have a particular Quarrel with Reason, Learning and Morality, for he seldom finished a Sermon without saying something against them.

   From such Men as these (*Whitefield* and *Tennant*) and such Doctrines and Ways of Preaching as theirs, what Fruit can you expect? Is it possible that the Exercise of Reason and Understanding should be promoted by such as make it their Business to vilify Reason and Understanding? Can solid and substantial Religion flow from superstitious, enthusiastick and nonsensical Preachers and Sermons? Can Charity the Queen of all the Graces be exalted by Slaves to Censoriousness, Hatred, and Evil-speaking? Can Patience, Meekness, Humility and other such Virtues be the Effects of Anger, Wrath, Pride, Arrogance, Impudence? As well may Light shine out of Darkness, or sweet Streams flow from a bitter Fountain. Indeed the People were roused and alarmed, and the general Cry was, *What shall we do to be saved?* But their Concern was wild, frantick, visionary, distracted and

[1]Imitator.

directed to false Methods of making their Peace with God, and attaining unto pure and undefiled Religion. As some People when their House is suddenly set on Fire, are greatly surprized, and run about with great Diligence to save their Goods, but throw their Glasses and other brittle Ware out at the Windows, whilst with great Care and Softness, they take up a joint Stool, and carry it out of Doors: So did the People here behave with respect to their Souls, when frightened and terrified by the Preaching of *Whitefield* and *Tennant*; they thought themselves in great Danger, they run Day and Night to Lectures, to Ministers, to private Meetings, to learn what they should do to be saved; but unhappily for them, they took up with the Show of Religion instead of the Substance; or they formed unworthy Notions of God and Virtue, instead of fixing in their Minds the rational and sublime Sentiments of the New Testament.

Accordingly the boasted Converts, not One of an Hundred excepted, make Religion to consist in the feeling of inward Impulses and Impressions, in an inexplicable Faith, Joys, Ecstasies, hearing of Sermons and such like Things. They are bigotted to certain Opinions which they do not understand, and have not the least Degree of Charity for those that are of another Way of thinking. They are all of them vain, self-conceited, superstitious, enthusiastick, censorious, Slanderers; Reason, Learning, Morality they professedly disregard: Should they hear a Minister preach in the most evangelical Manner upon any Moral Duty, or recommend the Exercise of Reason and Understanding, they would call him a dry, husky, *Arminian* Preacher, and conclude for certain that he was not converted. No Sermons please but such as move and heat the Passions, or scar and frighten them; solid Instruction is Heathen Morality, or carnal Preaching.

There has been great Confusion in the Churches: As soon as People are convicted, as the Phrase is, or converted, they become very turbulent, and disorderly. They give their Minister, if he is not of this new Way, a great deal of Trouble, and form Parties to turn him away from his Charge. Order, Regularity, Decency, and such Things, are made light of; and, in their Opinion, the more Confusion there is, the more there is of the Spirit of God amongst them. The Ministers here are divided, and look upon one another with an evil and jealous Eye. Several of them have rambled through the Country, after the Pattern of Mr. *Whitefield*, and without asking leave of the Minister of the Parish, have gathered the People together, and in a riotous manner entered the Meeting-house and preached. Very few Ministers have dared to open their Mouths in favour of Reason, Virtue, Order or anything that is thought to be against this Work. There is a Creature here whom perhaps you never heard of before. It is called *an Exhorter*. It is of both Sexes, but generally of the Male, and young. Its distinguishing Qualities are *Ignorance, Impudence, Zeal*. Numbers of these Exhorters are amongst the People here. They go from Town to Town, creep into Houses, lead Captive silly Women, and then the Men. Such of them as have good Voices do *great Execution*; they move their Hearers, make them cry, faint, swoon, fall into Convulsions. The converts are all made in this Manner; first, they become concerned for their Souls, and greatly distressed, and not rarely distracted. In this Condition they continue for some Days, and then all at once without any visible Means, they come out of their dark and disconsolate State, all Light, Joy, Ecstasy. This they express by their Talk to their Neighbours, which they call, telling their Experiences, and, in many Places, by immoderate Laughter, and singing of Hymns. Their Joy is sometimes so great, that their Eyes sparkle, and Faces shine, which are certain Signs of the Spirit of God's being in them.

There are many Lectures over all the Country on the Week-days; the People are more affected with these than with the Worship on the Sabbath-day. In many Towns at these Lectures, *Hundreds* have screamed out at once whilst the Minister was preaching, so that he has been obliged to leave off his Sermon and go down to the Persons in Distress and comfort them. But the *Exhorters* are the best beloved Creatures. The Ministers have generally endeavoured to preserve some kind of Order, and been satisfied with the crying out of a Number at the hearing of their Sermons; (the Minister that never made some body or other cry, is unconverted) but the Exhorters tarry in the Meeting-house with the People after the Minister is gone, and sometimes several of them [e]xhort at once in different Parts of the House, and then there is *terrible Doings*. You may hear Screaming, Singing, Laughing, Praying, all at once; and in other Parts they fall into Visions, Trances, Convulsions. When they come out of their Trances, they commonly tell a senseless Story of Heaven and Hell, and whom and what they saw there. In their Trances they neither hear, nor see, nor feel any more than if they were dead. There are several unaccountable Appearances whilst they are in these Fits, which the Converts impute to the Spirit of God, but which others ascribe to the Devil; but the wisest say are Effects of Disorders in the Brain or in the animal Spirits. In some Towns, several Persons, both Men and Women, that formerly were sober, and to all appearance truly pious, are raving distracted, so that they are confined and chained. Many fall into Epilepsies as they walk the Streets, or in their Houses. These Things are ascribed, and, I believe, with good Reason, to their continual Attention to one Set of Ideas, the Heat that is raised in their Imagination, Watchings, Fastings beyond Measure. They go about asking one another, *How do you feel? Have you seen Christ?* And if a Number of Converted meet together, they break out into a Laugh that surprizes every one, not infected with their Distemper. . . .

. . . [Davenport], whose Name you have no doubt seen in their printed Accounts of things, is so evidently distracted,[2] that was he in any sober Country in the World, he would be confined; and yet, in that Colony, he is attended with Crowds, and looked upon by Numbers as an Angel of God. In a hot Day, he strips to his Shirt, mounts a Cart, or any Eminence upon the Street, and roars and bellows, and flings about his Arms, till he is ready to drop down with the Violence of the Action.

The College in *Connecticut*[3] is broke up. The Students would neither mind their Studies, nor obey the Rules of the College. Almost all of them pretended to an inward Teacher which they ought to follow, and several of them made Excursions into the Country, and exhorted the People from Town to Town; so that the President was obliged to dismiss all of them from the College, and hath applied, as I heard, to the general Court, for Power to oblige the young Fellows to keep Order.

[2]Mentally ill.
[3]Yale.

20

BOSTON NEWS-LETTER

James Davenport's Arrest

1742

James Davenport (1716–1757), minister of Southold, Long Island, became one of the leading radical itinerants of the Great Awakening. Whereas his followers saw him as inspired by God, his detractors saw him as a fraud, or possibly even insane. In the hostile newspaper account

From *Boston News-Letter,* July 1, 1742.

excerpted here, Davenport's arrest under Connecticut's anti-itinerancy law is described in vivid detail.

Hartford, June 10, 1742

On the 27th of May last came certain Gentlemen of the parish of *Ripton* in the town of *Stratford*, and against said Mr. *Davenport* and one Mr. *Pom[e]roy* under their Hands; filed their complaint with the secretary, (the general assembly[1] then sitting) importing and setting forth, That about ten days before; came said Mr. *Davenport* to said *Stratford*, and soon after him said Mr. *Pom[e]roy*, and that they, together with certain illiterate persons, under colour[2] of preaching, praying and religious exhortations, and frequently congregating great numbers of persons, chiefly children & youth, did by sundry unwarrantable things, by them in an indecent and unjustifiable manner uttered and inculcated; put the said town, and especially said parish, into great confusion and disorder, and so for many days continued in a grievous manner to disturb the peace and quiet of his majesty's good subjects there, and thereupon praying relief in the premises.

On which representation, the question being put; Whether the things complained of were worthy the special notice and care of the assembly? was, by the concurrence of both houses, resolved in the affirmative. And thereupon, in the words following, *Ordered*, "That the secretary of this colony make out a precept, directed to the sheriff of the county of *Hartford* or his deputy, to arrest the bodies of *James Davenport* and *Benjamin Pom[e]roy*. . . ."

. . . I shall proceed to give you in substance from minutes taken at the time; 1. The *principal* and more *particular things* either evidenced or conceded to. And, 2[.] His *behaviour* and *treatment* during, and sundry *circumstances* attending, the agitation of these things.

I. The *particular & principal things* either evidenced or conceded to, were,

1. That speaking of his, & his adherents *conduct* and *doctrines* and the *effects* thereof in the land, and under the general character of, *This good work*; and speaking also of the *laws of the government* made, or about to be made, to regulate or restrain the same, he declared and insisted, that *all such laws ought to be disregarded*, and were *against the laws of GOD*.

[1] Elected legislature of the colony.
[2] Pretense.

2. That he earnestly inculcated it upon the minds of children and youth, that this work was the work of God, which they also were engaged in carrying on; and that all *prohibitions* and *commands of parents & masters* not to adhere to them, and attend their religious exercises, meetings, &c. were in *no wise to be obeyed.*

3. That he declared that *people ought not to regard or attend the preaching of unconverted ministers*; and that *he was well-assured the greater part of the ministers in the country were such.*

And, 4. That he endeavoured by *unwarrantable means* to *terrify* and *affect* his hearers. And that,

(1.) By pretending some *extraordinary discovery & assurance* of the very near approach of the *end of the world*; and that though he didn't assign the *very day*, yet that he then lately had it *clearly opened to him*, and *strongly impressed upon his mind*, that in a very *short time* all these things will be involved in devouring flames.—And also that on supposition & pretence of *extraordinary intercourse with heaven*, he frequently prayed for direction and acted in his undertakings.

(2.) By an *indecent and affected imitation* of the agony & passion of our blessed SAVIOUR; and also, by *voice* and *gesture*, of the surprize, horror and amazement of persons supposed to be sentenced to eternal misery. And,

(3.) By a *too peremptory & unconditioned* denouncing damnation against such of his auditory he looked upon as opposers; vehemently crying out, That *he saw hell-flames flashing in their faces*; and that *they were now! now! dropping down to hell*; and also added, *Lord! Thou knowest that there are many in that gallery and in these seats, that are now dropping down to Hell!* & etc.

5. It appeared also, That sundry of these things happened *unseasonably* and *late at night.*

II. Touching his *behaviour* and *treatment* during, and the *circumstances* attending, the agitation of these things, take as follows, *viz.*—On notice first given him by the sheriff of the will of the assembly, he showed himself thereto resigned, though just before, it seems had been determined to a different course by the special guidance of a superior authority.

On his arrival at *Hartford*, by the indulgence of the sheriff (who from first to last, treated and entertained at his own house, him and Mr. *Pom[e]roy*, with unexceptionable tenderness and civility) he spent the first night, and the greater part of the next day, among his special friends of followers, uninterrupted in religious Devotions; in his way:

by no means therein forgetting to vent the most virulent invectives against both ministers and magistrates, especially the general assembly, representing them as opposers of the work of God, and doing the work of the devil, & etc.

Nextly, view him at the bar of the assembly: his approach to which, his air and posture there; that inflexibility of body, that affectatious oblique reclining of the head, that elevation, or rather inversion of the eyes, that forced negligence and retirement of soul, and that uncouth show, that motley mixture of pride and gravity wrought up to sullenness, is not easily to be described. In this Posture view him invariable as a statue, 'till the adjournment and withdrawing of the assembly that evening; when, amid the thronging multitude (on that occasion very numerous) removed and moving out of the meeting-house, he and Mr. *Pom[e]roy* took their stand upon the assent to the front door, and there exhibited a lively specimen of their flaming zeal, or rather enthusiastic fury; many of the members of the general assembly then by.[3] With vehement stentorian voice, and wild distortions of body, said *Davenport* began an exhortation; on which the sheriff, by speaking and gently taking him by the sleeve, endeavouring to silence and remove him, he instantly fell a praying, crying out, *Lord! thou knowest somebody's got hold of my sleeve, strike them! Lord, strike them!*—which said *Pom[e]roy* also observing cried out to the sheriff and his assistants, *Take heed how you do that heaven-daring action! 'tis heaven-daring presumption to take him away! and the God of Heaven will assuredly avenge it on you! strike them, Lord, strike them!* many of the concourse beginning to sigh, groan, beat their breasts, cry out, and to be put into strange agitations of body. Others of their adherents rushing in violently interposed to prevent and resist the sheriff; while others refused their assistance when commanded, saying, *they were serving the devil*, & etc. 'til the tumult rose even to an uproar, which at length a little subsiding, the sheriff, with the two ministers, being about to retire to a gentleman's house hard by,[4] a multitude flocked after, some giving out and threatening, that the next day they should have five to one on their side, & etc.

But being gotten into said gentleman's house, and thither followed by a considerable number of their admirers, he, said *Davenport*, fell immediately to exhorting, and together with the rest, a praying, singing, &c. with much noise and vehemence; in which persisting;

[3]There.
[4]Nearby.

notwithstanding the repeated entreaties and prohibition of the master of the house, remonstrating it was a great Disturbance to his Family, some of them then a-bed, and ill able to endure the tumult.

Notwithstanding also the requests and the authoritative commands of the sheriff to forbear, still the hubbub increased; and in about two hours time was scarcely suppressed and dispersed by the interposition and authority of sundry of his majesty's council,[5] with the assistance of the sheriff, who, 'til then, had in vain attempted it.

In the mean time, almost all night, in other parts of the town, were such shocking scenes of horror and confusion, under the name and pretext of religious devotion, as language can't describe. Which wild ungovernable efforts of enthusiastic zeal and fury, being regarded as a bold and threatening insult upon the whole legislative body of the government, then on the spot; orders were forthwith given out to one of the commanding officers of the town, with about forty men in arms the next morning to wait upon the assembly; and so 'til the conclusion of these affairs: to prevent further insolences, which seemed to be threatening. Which orders were accordingly observed 'til the rising of the assembly.

[5]Members of the royal governing body.

21

The Testimony and Advice of an Assembly of Pastors

1743

A group of moderately pro-revival New England pastors met in Boston in 1743 and issued this guarded statement about the awakenings. They affirmed the revivals as godly on the whole but sternly warned against the radicals' excesses of uneducated preachers and exhorters, spiritual impulses, and church splits. They tried to chart a clear moderate position

From *The Testimony and Advice of an Assembly of Pastors of Churches in New-England* (Boston, 1743), 5–12.

between antirevivalists such as Charles Chauncy and radicals such as James Davenport.

When CHRIST is pleased to come into his Church in a plentiful Effusion of his Holy Spirit, by whose powerful Influences the Ministration of the Word is attended with uncommon Success, Salvation-Work carried on in an eminent Manner, and his Kingdom, which is *within Men*, and consists in *Righteousness and Peace and Joy in the Holy Ghost*, is notably advanced, — THIS is an Event which above all other invites the Notice, and bespeaks the Praises of the Lord's People, and should be declared abroad for a *Memorial* of the divine Grace, — as it tends to enliven the Prayers, strengthen the Faith, and raise the Hopes, of such as are *waiting for the Kingdom of God*, and the coming on of the Glory of the latter Days. . . .

. . . We, whose Names are hereunto annexed, Pastors of Churches in *New-England*, met together in *Boston*, July 7th 1743, think it *our* indispensable Duty, (without judging or censuring such of our Brethren as cannot at present see Things in the same Light with us) in this open and conjunct Manner to declare, to the Glory of sovereign Grace, our full Perswasion, either from what we have seen our selves, or received upon credible Testimony, That there has been a *happy* and *remarkable Revival of Religion in many Parts of this Land, thro' an uncommon divine Influence*; after a long Time of great Decay and Deadness, and a sensible and very awful Withdraw of the Holy Spirit from his Sanctuary among us. . . .

. . . The *present Work* appears to be remarkable and extraordinary,

On Account of the *Numbers wrought upon* — We never before saw so many brought under Soul-Concern, and with Distress making the Inquiry, *What must we do to be saved?* And these Persons of all Characters and Ages. — With Regard to the *Suddenness* and *quick Progress* of it — Many Persons and Places were surprized with the gracious Visit together, or near about the same Time; and the heavenly Influence diffused itself far and wide like the Light of the Morning. — Also in Respect of the *Degree of Operation*, both in a Way of *Terror* and in a Way of *Consolation*; attended in many with unusual *bodily Effects*. —

Not that all who are accounted the Subjects of the present Work, have had these extraordinary Degrees of previous Distress and subsequent Joy. But many, and we suppose the greater Number, have been wrought on in a more gentle and silent Way, and without any other

Appearances than are common and usual at other Times, when Persons have been awakened to a solemn Concern about Salvation, and have been thought to have passed out of a State of Nature into a State of Grace.

As to those whose *inward Concern* has occasioned extraordinary *outward Distresses*, the most of them when we came to converse with them, were able to give, what appeared to us, a rational Account of what so affected their Minds; *viz.* A quick Sense of their *Guilt, Misery* and *Danger*; and they would often mention the Passages in the Sermons they heard, or particular Texts of Scripture, which were set home upon them with such a powerful Impression. — And as to such whose *Joys* have carried them into *Transports* and *Ecstasies*, they in like Manner have accounted for *them*, from a lively Sense of the Danger they hoped they were freed from, and the Happiness they were now possessed of; such clear Views of divine and heavenly Things, and particularly of the Excellencies and Loveliness of JESUS CHRIST, and such sweet Tastes of redeeming Love as they never had before. — The Instances were very few in which we had Reason to think these Affections were produced by *visionary* or sensible Representations, or by any other Images than such as the Scripture it self presents unto us.

And here we think it not amiss to declare, that in dealing with these Persons we have been careful to inform them, That the Nature of Conversion does not consist in these passionate Feelings; and to warn them not to look upon their State safe, because they have passed out of deep Distress into high Joys, unless they experience a Renovation of Nature, followed with a Change of Life, and a Course of vital Holiness. — Nor have we gone into such an Opinion of the *bodily Effects* with which this Work has been attended in some of its Subjects, as to judge them any Signs that Persons who have been so affected, were *then* under a *saving Work* of the Spirit of God. No; we never so much as called these bodily Seizures, *Convictions*; or spoke of them as the *immediate* Work of the Holy Spirit. Yet we do not think them inconsistent with a Work of GOD upon the Soul at that very Time; but judge that those inward Impressions which come from the Spirit of GOD, those Terrors and Consolations of which He is the Author, may, according to the natural Frame and Constitution which some Persons are of, occasion such bodily Effects. — And therefore that these extraordinary outward Symptoms, are not an Argument that the Work is delusive, or from the Influence and Agency of the evil Spirit.

With Respect to Numbers of those who have been under the Impressions of the present Day, we must declare there is good Ground to conclude they are become *real Christians*. . . .

Indeed many who appeared to be under Convictions, and were much altered in their external Behaviour, when this Work began, and while it was most flourishing, have lost their Impressions, and are relapsed into their former Manner of Life: Yet of those who were judged hopefully converted, and made a publick Profession of Religion, there have been *fewer Instances* of *Scandal* and *Apostasy* than might be expected. — So that, as far as we are able to form a Judgment, the Face of Religion is lately changed much for the better in many of our Towns and Congregations; and together with a *Reformation* observable in diverse Instances, there appears to be more *experimental Godliness*, and *lively Christianity*, than the most of us can remember we have ever seen before. —

. . . We must necessarily be grieved at any Accounts sent abroad, representing this Work as all *Enthusiasm, Delusion* and *Disorder.* —

Indeed it is not to be denied that in some Places many Irregularities and Extravagancies have been permitted to accompany it, which we would deeply lament and bewail before GOD, and look upon our selves obliged, for the Honour of the HOLY SPIRIT, and of his blessed Operations on the Souls of Men, to bear a publick and faithful Testimony against; though at the same Time it is to be acknowledged with much Thankfulness, that in *other Places*, where the Work has greatly flourished, there have been few if any of these Disorders and Excesses. — But who can wonder, if at such a Time as this Satan should intermingle himself, to hinder and blemish a Work so directly contrary to the Interests of his own Kingdom? — Or, if while so much good Seed is sowing, *the Enemy should be busy to sow Tares?*[1] — We would therefore, in the *Bowels of Jesus*, beseech such as have been Partakers of this Work, or are zealous to promote it, that they *be not ignorant of* Satan's *Devices*; that they *watch* and *pray* against Errors & Misconduct of every Kind, lest they blemish and hinder that which they desire to honour and advance. — Particularly,

That they do not make *secret Impulses* on their Minds, without a due Regard to the *written Word*, the Rule of their Duty. . . . That *Laymen* do not invade the Ministerial Office, and under a Pretence of *Exhorting* set up *Preaching*; which is very contrary to Gospel Order, and tends to introduce Errors and Confusion into the Church. — That *Ministers* do not invade the Province of others, and in *ordinary Cases*

---

[1]"Tares" are weeds.

preach in another's Parish without his Knowledge, and against his Consent: Nor encourage *raw* and *indiscreet* young *Candidates*, in rushing into particular Places, and preaching publickly or privately, as some have done to the no small Disrepute and Damage of the Work in Places where it once promised to flourish. Though at the same Time we would have Ministers show their Regard to the spiritual Welfare of their People, by suffering them to partake of the Gifts and Graces of *able, sound* and *zealous Preachers of the Word*, as GOD in his Providence may give Opportunity [for]: Being persuaded GOD has in this Day remarkably blessed the Labours of *some* of his Servants who have *travelled* in preaching the Gospel of CHRIST.—That People beware of entertaining Prejudices against their *own Pastors*, and don't run into *unscriptural* Separations.—That they don't indulge a *disputatious Spirit*, which has been attended with mischievous Effects; nor discover a Spirit of *Censoriousness, Uncharitableness*, and rash *judging* the State of others; than which scarce any Thing has more blemished the Work of GOD amongst us.—And while we would meekly *exhort* both Ministers and Christians, so far as is consistent with *Truth* and *Holiness*, to *follow the Things that make for Peace*; we would most earnestly *warn* all Sorts of Persons not to *despise* these Out-pourings of the Spirit, lest a holy GOD be provoked to withhold them, and instead thereof to pour out upon this People the Vials of his Wrath, in temporal Judgments and spiritual Plagues; and would *call* upon every one to improve this remarkable Season of Grace, and put in for a Share of the heavenly Blessings so liberally dispensed.—

Finally,

We exhort the Children of GOD to *continue instant*[2] *in Prayer*, that He, with whom is *the Residue of the Spirit*, would grant us fresh, more plentiful and extensive Effusions, that so this Wilderness, in all the Parts of it, may become a fruitful Field:—That the present Appearances may be an *Earnest*[3] of the glorious Things promised to the Church in the latter Days; when she shall *shine with the Glory of the LORD arisen upon her*, so as to dazzle the Eyes of Beholders, confound and put to Shame all her Enemies, rejoice the Hearts of her solicitous and now saddened Friends, and have a strong Influence and Resplendency throughout the Earth.—*AMEN! Even so come LORD JESUS; Come quickly!*

[2]Engaged.
[3]Preview.

22

BOSTON EVENING-POST

James Davenport's Book and Clothes Burning

1743

Davenport's arrests in Hartford and Boston made him the most notorious evangelical in New England and the focal point of much of the controversy regarding the revivals. Then, in 1743, he reappeared in New London, Connecticut. The hostile newspaper account excerpted here described how Davenport's radical followers burned copies of well-regarded Christian authors' books. It was no surprise that Davenport called on the crowd to burn the works of Charles Chauncy, the chief anti-revivalist writer in New England. He also consigned older devotional classics, such as those of the seventeenth-century Puritan writer John Flavel, to the flames, presumably because he judged them theologically deficient or too focused on good works instead of God's grace. Finally, he burned the works of moderate evangelical leaders such as Boston's Benjamin Colman and New London's Eliphalet Adams, both of whom Davenport regarded as insufficiently supportive of the awakenings and unconverted. Davenport's friends stopped short the next day, however, when he called on them to burn their fancy clothes.

The *Separatists* at *New-London* sent a Boat over to *Long Island* to invite the grand Enthusiast *Davenport* over to Organize their Church (as they termed it). He arrived on or about the second Day of *March*: He was no sooner come to Town, than he began to rectify some Disorders he supposed were prevailing among the Children of God: He published the Messages which he said he received from the Spirit in Dreams and otherwise, importing the great Necessity of Mortification and *contempt* of the World; and made them believe that they must put away from them every thing that they delighted in, to avoid the Heinous Sin of Idolatry,[1] that Wigs, Cloaks and Breeches, Hoods,

---

[1]Worshipping anything above God.

From *Boston Evening-Post*, April 11, 1743.

Gowns, Rings, Jewels and Necklaces must be all brought together into one Heap into his Chamber, that they might by his solemn Decree be committed to the Flames; together with certain Books of Devotion, & etc. which he determined to be unsafe to be in the Hands of the People. Accordingly, they seemed to be in a Strife who should be first in this meritorious Action, and then was presently made a Pile of Men's and Women's Apparel and Ornaments to which the grand Director added a pair of Plush Breeches which he wore to Town, and which now he would greatly want, were he not confined in Bed by a Distemper for which I want a Name. A *New-Light* Physician who attends him, (and no other may come nigh[2] him) says it is the *Canker*, and sure it eats like one, and is supposed by others to be what may be termed the *Grand Scurvy*.

The Books which were committed to the Flames were as follows, *Beveridge's* Thoughts on Religion, part of *Flavel's* Works, one piece of Mr. *Henry's*, *Russel's* seven Sermons, *Dyer's* Golden Chain, the Whole Duty of Man, one piece of Dr. *Increase Mather*, one of Dr. *Colman's*, one of Dr. *Sewall's*, and Dr. *Chauncy's* Sermon against Enthusiasm, Mr. *Adams's* Sermons, all that could be had; *Flynt's* 20 Sermons, *Barnard's*, *Hooper's*, *Hart's*, *Samuel Russel's*, *Beckworth's*, *Todd's*, *Seaberry's* and *Bliss's* Sermons, with a Book of *Williams* and *Wadsworth*; these being called over, were with much Noise and Outcry burnt on the Town Wharf in the Afternoon of the Sabbath Day, *March* 6th. just as People were coming from Meeting, who ran to see if Murder or some other Mischief was not about to be done, and so were Witnesses of this their horrid Delusion, and heard them sing *Hallelujahs* and *Gloria Patri* over the Pile, and heard them with a loud Voice declare, *That the Smoke of the Torments of such of the Authors of the abovesaid Books as died in the same Belief as when they set them out, was now ascending in Hell in like Manner as they saw the Smoke of them Books rise.* The next Day sundry other Books (to me unknown) were burnt, and the Clothes, & etc. which were ready in a Pile for that Purpose, would certainly have been consumed, but that one of the Fraternity who loved the World better than the rest, and was more apprehensive of the ill Aspect this Transaction would have on their Scheme and Party, came running and diverted them from it for that Time; and thus having Time to consider a little, one of the Female Bigots drew back her Cloak, saying, *The Calf you have made[3] is too big*, and flung *Daven-*

---

[2]Near.
[3]Refers to the idol in the form of a golden calf made by the Israelites in Exodus 32.

port's Plush Breeches into his Face; and being further told that this their Conduct would destroy their Scheme, and ruin their Interest among the People, they judged some Retraction necessary, and so they declared publickly against what had been done, as the Fruit of a Delusion; and even the Ringleader himself declared the same, and then they fell to confessing their Sins publickly; one told of one Thing, and another of another, many of them declaring they believed they were *Judas's;*[4] and one of the Armour-bearers[5] said, that he had depended upon it[6] he had been in Christ for the Space of *three Years*, but now he believed he was a *Judas*, and was come over to the Main to be a Spectacle, should be hanged up and his Bowels would gush out.[7]

[4]Judas was the disciple who betrayed Jesus.
[5]Davenport apparently had specially chosen followers he called "armor-bearers," recalling 1 Samuel 16, in which David becomes King Saul's armor-bearer.
[6]Believed.
[7]Judas's fate in Matthew 27:3 and Acts 1:18.

23

JAMES DAVENPORT

Confession and Retractions

1744

After Davenport's book-burning debacle, he sought to resurrect his career and reputation among moderate evangelicals. In this excerpt, Davenport explains that he had made certain mistakes but that they did not compromise the legitimacy of the Great Awakening or his own ministry as a whole. Davenport blamed his conduct at the book and clothes burning on a canker, or ulcer, in his leg that led him into a feverish delirium. Some critics, of course, found his apology unconvincing. Davenport maintained a much more moderate style for the remainder of his pastoral career, which continued in New England and the Middle Colonies until his death in 1757.

From James Davenport, *The Reverend Mr. Davenport's Confession and Retractions* (Boston, 1744), 3–8.

Although I don't question at all, but there is great Reason to bless God for a *glorious and wonderful Work of his Power and Grace* in the *Edification* of his Children, and the *Conviction* and *Conversion* of Numbers in *New-England*, in the *neighbouring Governments* and *several other Parts*, within a few Years past; and believe that the Lord hath favoured me, though most unworthy, with several others of his Servants, in granting special Assistance and Success; the Glory of all which be given to JEHOVAH, to whom alone it belongs:

Yet after frequent Meditation and Desires that I might be enabled to apprehend Things justly, and, I hope I may say, mature Consideration; I am now fully convinced and persuaded that *several Appendages* to *this glorious Work* are no essential Parts thereof, but of a *different* and *contrary* Nature and Tendency; *which Appendages* I have been in the Time of the Work very industrious in and instrumental of promoting, by a misguided Zeal: being further much influenced in the Affair by the *false Spirit*; which, unobserved by me, did (as I have been brought to see since) prompt me to *unjust Apprehensions* and *Misconduct* in *several Articles*; which have been great Blemishes to the Work of God. . . .

The *Articles*, which I especially refer to, and would in the most public Manner *retract*, and *warn others against*, are these which follow, *viz.*

I. The Method I used for a considerable Time, with Respect to some, yea many *Ministers* in several Parts, in openly *exposing such as I feared or thought unconverted, in public Prayer or otherwise*: herein making my private Judgment, (in which also I much suspect I was mistaken in several Instances, and I believe also that my Judgment concerning several, was formed rashly and upon very slender Grounds.) I say making my private Judgment, the Ground of public Actions or Conduct. . . .

II. By my *advising and urging to such Separations* from *those Ministers*, whom I treated as above, as I believe may justly be called rash, unwarrantable, and of sad and awful Tendency and Consequence. And here I would ask the Forgiveness of those Ministers, whom I have injured in both these Articles.

III. I confess I have been much led astray by *following Impulses* or Impressions as a Rule of Conduct, whether they came with or without a Text of Scripture; and my neglecting also duly to observe the Analogy of Scripture: I am persuaded this was a great Means of corrupting my Experiences and carrying me off from the Word of God, and a great Handle, which the *false Spirit* has made use of with Respect to a Number, and me especially.

IV. I believe further that I have done much Hurt to Religion by *encouraging private Persons to a ministerial and authoritative Kind or Method of exhorting*; which is particularly observable in many such being much puffed up and *falling into the Snare of the Devil,* while many others are thus directly prejudiced against the Work.

V. I have Reason to be deeply humbled that I have not been duly careful to endeavour to remove or prevent Prejudice, (where I now believe I might then have done it consistently with Duty) which appeared remarkable in the Method I practiced, of *singing with others in the Streets* in Societies frequently.

I would also penitently confess and bewail my *great Stiffness* in retaining these *aforesaid Errors* a great while, and Unwillingness to examine into them with any Jealousy of their being Errors, notwithstanding the friendly Counsels and Cautions of real Friends, especially in the Ministry.

Here may properly be added a Paragraph or two, taken out of a *Letter from me* to Mr. *Barber* at *Georgia*; a *true Copy* of which I gave Consent should be published lately at *Philadelphia*: "—I would add to what Brother *T[ennent]* hath written on the awful Affair of Books and Clothes at *New-London*, which affords Grounds of deep and lasting Humiliation; I was to my Shame be it spoken, the Ringleader in *that horrid Action*; I was, my dear Brother, under the powerful Influence of the *false Spirit* almost one whole Day together, and Part of several Days. The Lord showed me afterwards that the Spirit I was then acted by was in it's Operations void of true inward Peace, laying the greatest Stress on Externals, neglecting the Heart, full of Impatience, Pride and Arrogance; although I thought in the Time of it, that it was the Spirit of God in an high Degree; awful indeed! my Body especially my Leg much disordered at the same Time,[1] which Satan and my evil Heart might make some Handle of. —"

---

[1] I had the *long Fever* on me and the cankry Humour raging at once. [Davenport]

5
Evangelicals in the South

24

GEORGE WHITEFIELD

To the Inhabitants of Maryland, Virginia, North and South-Carolina
1740

As we saw in Josiah Smith's sermon on Whitefield (see Document 5), he had a number of friends in the South. He did nothing to help his reputation among white slaveholders, however, with this 1740 letter chastising slave owners for their abuse of their slaves. Lest we think that Whitefield was unusually progressive in his views on slavery, we should remember that he was not opposed to slavery itself and later became a slave owner. He did, however, see African Americans as needing the new birth, and so he encouraged masters to teach them about Christianity, as this excerpt shows.

As I lately passed through your Provinces in my Way hither, I was sensibly touched with a Fellow-feeling of the Miseries of the poor Negroes. Could I have preached more frequently amongst you, I should have delivered my Thoughts in my publick Discourses; but as my Business here required me to stop as little as possible on the Road, I have no other Way to discharge the Concern which at present lies upon my Heart, than by sending you this Letter: How you will

From George Whitefield, "To the Inhabitants of Maryland, Virginia, North and South-Carolina," in *Three Letters from the Reverend Mr. G. Whitefield* (Philadelphia, 1740), 13–15.

receive it I know not; whether you will accept it in Love, or be offended with me . . . I am uncertain. Whatever be the Event, I must inform you in the Meekness and Gentleness of *Christ*, that I think God has a Quarrel with you for your Abuse of and Cruelty to the poor Negroes. Whether it be lawful for Christians to buy Slaves, and thereby encourage the Nations from whom they are bought, to be at perpetual War with each other, I shall not take upon me to determine; sure I am, it is sinful, when bought, to use them as bad, nay worse, than as though they were Brutes; and whatever particular Exceptions there may be (as I would charitably hope there are some) I fear the Generality of you that own Negroes, are liable to such a Charge; for your Slaves, I believe, work as hard if not harder than the Horses whereon you ride.

These, after they have done their Work, are fed and taken proper Care of; but many Negroes when wearied with Labour in your Plantations, have been obliged to grind their own Corn after they return home.

Your Dogs are caressed and fondled at your Tables: But your Slaves, who are frequently styled Dogs or Beasts, have not an equal Privilege. They are scarce permitted to pick up the Crumbs which fall from their Masters' Tables. Nay, some, as I have been informed by an Eye-Witness, have been, upon the most trifling Provocation, cut with Knives, and had Forks thrown into their Flesh — Not to mention what Numbers have been given up to the inhuman Usage of cruel Task Masters, who by their unrelenting Scourges have ploughed upon their Backs, and made long Furrows, and at length brought them even to Death itself.

It's true, I hope there are but few such Monsters of Barbarity suffered[1] to subsist amongst you. Some, I hear, have been lately executed in *Virginia* for killing Slaves, and the Laws are very severe against such who at any Time murder them.

And perhaps it might be better for the poor Creatures themselves, to be hurried out of Life, than to be made so miserable, as they generally are in it. And indeed, considering what Usage they commonly meet with, I have wondered, that we have not more Instances of Self-Murder among the Negroes, or that they have not more frequently rose up in Arms against their Owners. *Virginia* has once, and *Charlestown* [South Carolina] more than once been threatened in this Way.

---

[1]Allowed.

. . . For God is the same to Day as he was Yesterday, and will continue the same forever.[2] He does not reject the Prayer of the poor and destitute, nor disregard the Cry of the meanest Negroes! . . . But this is not all—Enslaving or misusing their Bodies would, comparatively speaking, be an inconsiderable Evil, was proper Care taken of their Souls. But I have great reason to believe, that most of you, on Purpose, keep your Negroes ignorant of Christianity; or otherwise, why are they permitted through your Provinces, openly to profane the Lord's Day, by their Dancing, Piping and such like? I know the general Pretence for this Neglect of their Souls is, That teaching them Christianity would make them proud, and consequently unwilling to submit to Slavery: But what a dreadful Reflection is this on your Holy Religion? What blasphemous Notions must those that make such an Objection have of the Precepts of Christianity? Do you find any one Command in the Gospel, that has the least Tendency to make People forget their relative Duties? Do you not read that Servants, and as many as are under the Yoke of Bondage, are required to be subject, in all lawful Things, to their Masters; and that not only to the good and gentle, but also to the froward?[3] . . . I challenge the whole World to produce a single Instance of a Negroe's being made a thorough Christian, and thereby made a worse Servant. It cannot be.—But farther, if teaching Slaves Christianity has such a bad Influence upon their Lives, why are you generally desirous of having your Children taught? Think you they are any way better by Nature than the poor Negroes? No, in no wise. Blacks are just as much, and no more, conceived and born in Sin, as White Men are. Both, if born and bred up here, I am persuaded, are naturally capable of the same Improvement.—And as for the grown Negroes, I am apt to think, whenever the Gospel is preached with Power amongst them, that many will be brought effectually home to God. Your present and past bad Usage of them, however ill-designed, may thus far do them good, as to break their Wills, increase the Sense of their natural Misery, and consequently better dispose their Minds to accept the Redemption wrought out for them, by the Death and Obedience of Jesus Christ. God has, not long since, been pleased to make some of the Negroes in *New-England*, Vessels of Mercy; and some of them, I hear, have been brought to cry out, *What shall we do*

[2]Hebrews 13:8.
[3]"Froward" means unreasonable. The reference here is to 1 Peter 2:18.

to be saved? in the Province of *Pennsylvania.* Doubtless there is a Time, when the Fullness of the Gentiles will come in:[4] And then I believe, if not before, these despised Slaves will find the Gospel of Christ to be the Power of God to their Salvation, as well as we.

[4]Romans 11:25. Whitefield believed that some African Americans would be part of the Gentiles (non-Jews) whom God would choose for salvation.

25

BOSTON POST-BOY

Hugh Bryan's Radicalism

1742

Hugh Bryan (d. 1753) and his brother Jonathan were wealthy South Carolina planters who experienced the new birth under Whitefield's preaching. As this newspaper account describes, the early years of his converted life led Hugh into radical ideas that he might become a prophet who would lead the slaves out of captivity. He began holding illegal meetings with slaves, suggesting that they might rise up against South Carolina slaveholders. Bryan's prophetic career came to an abrupt end, however, when he tried to part the waters of a river. He soon moderated his ideas significantly and continued to own slaves, but he also continued to work toward evangelizing the slaves of South Carolina.

I Sent you *per* last, some Specimens of our prophetick Predictions in the Province, the grand Prophet (*Hugh Bryan*) at last sent a whole Volume of his Prophecies (containing as much horrid Blasphemy and Nonsense as can be contained in 20 Sheets of Paper close written) directed to the Speaker of Commons House of Assembly. This, together with certain Advices of his being encamped in the Wilderness, and gathering considerable Number of all Sorts of People about

From *Boston Post-Boy*, May 3, 1742.

him, specially Negroes, roused our Government, so that Warrants were immediately issued for apprehending him, but lo! Before the Officers could arrive at the Place (50 Miles from *Charlestown*) a strange Revolution had come over our Prophet; for (as you'll see by his Letter in the Print, I herewith send you) he had found out, that all his Prophecies had been inspired, not by the Spirit of GOD, but by the Devil himself only. The Way or Means how he came at this Discovery, he does not say in his Letter; but which his own Brother, who attended him in all his Adventures, relates thus;

"The invisible Spirit, with which he conversed so familiarly for many Days, directed him to go and take him a Rod, of such a certain Shape and Dimensions, from such a Tree, in such a Place as he told him of; and therewith to go and smite the Waters of the River, which should thereby be divided, so as he might go over, on dry Ground. Away he hastens immediately to find the Tree, in a direct Course, through thick and thin; and being forbidden to look on the Ground, with two or three Tumbles-down in the Way, he finds the Tree, cuts him thence a Rod, of the proper Shape and Dimensions; and away he drives full Tilt with it into the River, and falls a smiting, splashing and spluttering the Water about with it, till he was quite up to the Chin; and his Brother, who had pursued him as fast as he could had enough to do to save him from being drowned. This Affair turning out so badly, his Brother presses him to return Home: But no; The Spirit had assured him, that if he went Home that Night, he should be a dead Man before next Morning: However, Much pressing, sharp Weather and a Wet Jacket, at length prevailed: Home he went, slept at Home that Night; and yet found himself alive next Morning. These Two notable Events opened his Eyes, and occasioned his grand Discovery."

Lo! *Dear Sir,* The Workings of Whit[e]fieldism in its native Tendency, got to its *ne plus ultra*[1] among the few remaining Proselytes in this Province; and I doubt not will soon arrive to some pitch in Yours. I pray GOD to preserve from tragic Events.

[1]Highest level.

26

SAMUEL DAVIES

On Virginia's Christian Slaves

1757

Presbyterian minister Samuel Davies (1723–1761) arrived in Hanover County, Virginia, in 1747. There he showed great interest not only in his white parishioners but also in their slaves. In a letter to his English benefactors, excerpted here, Davies described his observations of the slaves' religious lives and his integration of slaves into his church services. He also assured contributors that Christianizing the slaves would help keep them on the British side in the Seven Years' War (known as the French and Indian War in America). That war had begun in America only three years earlier.

I count myself happy, Sir, that I can retaliate[1] you, and the other Benefactors of this scheme, in that way, in which only you desire it; and that is, by giving you an account of the *Distribution* and *Acceptance of the books* among those, for whom they were intended. . . .

When the books arrived, I gave public notice of it, after Sermon, at the next opportunity: I desired such *Negroes* as could read, and also such *white* People as would make a *good use* of them, and were so *poor*, that they could not buy such books, to come to me at my house, and I should distribute them among them. On this occasion, I also enlarged upon a new topic of conviction both to the *Slaves* themselves, and their *Masters*.

"Since persons at so great a distance, who had no connection with them, were so generously concerned to christianize the poor *Negroes*, and had been at so much pains and expense for that end; then, how much more concerned, how much more zealous and industrious should their *Masters* be, to whom the care of their souls, as well as their bodies, is committed, and who enjoy the advantage of their laborious service?—And how much more ought the *poor Negroes* to be

[1]Repay.

From Samuel Davies, *Letters from the Rev. Samuel Davies* (London, 1757), 15–19.

concerned for themselves? And how much more aggravated would be their guilt and ruin, if they persisted in obstinate infidelity and wickedness, after so much pains had been taken with them for their conversion?" This, as I found afterwards, proved a very popular topic of conviction, and made some impressions upon the minds of not a few.

For some time after this, the *poor Slaves*, whenever they could get an hour's leisure from their masters, would hurry away to my house; and received the Charity with all the genuine indications of passionate gratitude, which unpolished nature could give; and which affectation and grimace would mimic in vain. The books were all *very acceptable*; but none more so than the *Psalms* and *Hymns*, which enabled them to gratify their peculiar taste for *Psalmody*. Sundry of them have lodged all night in my kitchen; and, sometimes, when I have awaked about two or three a-clock in the morning, a torrent of sacred harmony poured into my chamber, and carried my mind away to Heaven. In this seraphic exercise, some of them spend almost the whole night. . . .

The *good effects* of this pious Charity are already apparent. It convinces the *Heathen*, that however vicious, and careless about the Religion they profess, the generality of the white People are; yet, there are some who really look upon it as a matter of the utmost importance, and universal concern, and are actuated with a disinterested zeal to promote it — It has excited some of their *Masters* to emulation; and they are ashamed that *Strangers*, on the other side the *Atlantic*, should be at the pains to teach their domestics Christianity, and they should be quite negligent *themselves* — It furnishes the most proper helps for such *Negroes* as can read, and are piously disposed; and some of them are evidently improving in knowledge. . . .

This CHARITY may also be of singular service in a POLITICAL View; for now, when the *French* and *Indians* are invading our country, and perpetrating the most shocking barbarities and depredations upon our frontiers, we have not been without alarming apprehensions of Insurrection and Massacre, from the *numerous Slaves* among ourselves, whom they might seduce to their interest by the delusive promises of Liberty. And while they do not feel the restraints of Conscience and Christianity, our apprehensions are but too well grounded. I have done my utmost, without hinting my design to them, to prevent so dismal a calamity; and for this purpose, I have endeavoured to convince them, that there are many of the *English*, as well as myself, who are really solicitous for their welfare, which has given me no small popularity among them; and especially to bring them under the restraints of the pacific Religion of JESUS, which has so friendly an influence upon society, and teaches a proper conduct for every station in life. Now I can distribute these books among them as tokens of disinterested benevolence, as helps to understand Christianity, and in the mean time to detect the Impostures, Superstitions and Cruelties of POPERY.[2] . . .

There are *thousands of Negroes* in this colony, who still continue in the grossest ignorance, and most stupid carelessness about Religion, and as rank *Pagans*, as when they left the wilds of *Africa*. And there are not a few of this unhappy character, even in the bounds of my congregation; (which, by the by, is about sixty miles in circumference). But I think, Sir, my ministry of late has been most successful among them. Two *Sundays* ago, I had the pleasure of seeing *forty* of their black faces around the Table of the Lord, who all make a credible profession of Christianity, and sundry of them with unusual evidences of sincerity.

Last *Sunday*, I baptized *seven* or *eight Adults*, who had been Catechumens[3] for some time. Indeed, many of them seem determined to press into the kingdom of God; and, I am persuaded, will find an abundant entrance, when many of the children of the kingdom shall be shut out—*One* of the Catechumens baptized last *Sunday*, I conversed with the evening before; he addressed me to this purpose in broken *English*, "I am a poor slave, brought into a strange country, where I never expect to enjoy my liberty. While I lived in my own country, I knew nothing of that JESUS I have heard you speak so much about. I lived quite careless what will become of me when I die; but I now see such a life will never do, and I come to you, Sir, that you may tell me some good things, concerning JESUS CHRIST, and my Duty to GOD, for I am resolved not to live any more as I have done." Such a simple address is very striking oratory to me; and would my time allow, I could give you many such specimens.

[2]"Popery" is a disparaging term for Roman Catholicism, the religious affiliation of the French, whom the British were fighting in the Seven Years' War.
[3]People receiving instruction in preparation for baptism.

27

CHARLES WOODMASON

Evangelicals in the Southern Backcountry
1767–1768

Charles Woodmason (b. 1720?) was a non-evangelical Anglican ("Episcopal") itinerant in the southern backcountry who deplored the influence of the evangelical churches and itinerants he encountered. As these selections from his journal indicate, he saw the evangelicals— "Baptists, New Lights, Presbyterians, Independants, and an hundred other Sects"— as fractious and chaotic, and took deep personal offense at their attacks on him. By contrast, many in the rough-and-tumble world of the backcountry saw the evangelicals as offering pastoral attention and warm community in a region that sorely lacked both.

Sunday January 25, 1767
A Congregation at the Cheraws[1] of above 500 People. Baptiz'd about 60 Children—Quite jaded out[2]—standing and speaking 6 Hours together and nothing to refresh me, but Water—and their Provisions I could not touch—All the Cookery of these People being exceeding filthy, and most execrable.

Next Day, I returned and preached the 27th in my Way back at Lynch's Creek to a great Multitude of People assembled together, being the 1st Episcopal Minister they had seen since their being in the province—They complain'd of being eaten up by Itinerant Teachers, Preachers, and Imposters from New England and Pensylvania— Baptists, New Lights, Presbyterians, Independants, and an hundred other Sects—So that one day You might hear this System of Doctrine—the next day another—next day another, retrograde to both— Thus by the Variety of Taylors who would pretend to know the best

---

[1] In north-central South Carolina.
[2] Exhausted.

From Richard J. Hooker, ed., *The Carolina Backcountry on the Eve of the Revolution: The Journal and Other Writings of Charles Woodmason, Anglican Itinerant* (Chapel Hill: University of North Carolina Press, 1953), 13, 45, 101–3.

fashion in which Christs Coat is to be worn none will put it on—And among the Various Plans of Religion, they are at Loss which to adapt, and consequently are without any Religion at all. They came to Sermon with Itching Ears only, not with any Disposition of Heart, or Sentiment of mind—Assemble out of Curiousity, not Devotion, and seem so pleas'd with their native Ignorance, as to be offended at any Attempts to rouse them out of it.— ...

Not long after, they hir'd a Band of rude fellows to come to Service who brought with them 57 Dogs (for I counted them) which in Time of Service they set fighting, and I was obliged to stop—In Time of Sermon they repeated it—and I was oblig'd to desist and dismiss the People. It is in vain to take up or commit these lawless Ruffians—for they have nothing, and the Charge of sending of them to Charlestown,[3] would take me a Years Salary—We are without any Law, or Order—And as all the Magistrates are Presbyterians, I could not get a Warrant—If I got Warrants as the Constables are Presbyterians likewise, I could not get them serv'd—If serv'd, the Guard would let them escape—Both my Self and other Episcopals have made this Experiment—They have granted me Writs thro' fear of being complain'd off, but took Care not to have them serv'd—I took up one fellow for a Riot at a Wedding, and creating disturbance—The people took up two others for entering the House where I was when in Bed—stealing my Gown—putting it on—and then visiting a Woman in Bed, and getting to Bed to her, and making her give out next day, that the Parson came to Bed to her—This was a Scheme laid by the Baptists—and Man and Woman prepared for the Purpose. The People likewise took up some others for calling of me Jesuit,[4] and railing against the Service—The Constable let them all loose—No bringing of them to Justice—I enter'd Informations against some Magistrates for marrying—but cannot get them out of the other Justices Hands till too late to send to Town for a Judges Warrant.

Another Time (in order to disapoint me of a Congregation, and to laugh at the People) they posted a Paper, signifying, That the King having discovered the Popish Designs of Mr. Woodmason and other Romish Priests in disguise, to bring in Popery and Slavery, had sent over Orders to suspend them all, and to order them to be sent over to England, so that there would be no more preaching for the future.

---

[3]They were sent there for trial.
[4]A member of a Catholic missionary order.

This was believed by some of the Poor Ignorants, and kept them at home. . . .

For only draw a Comparison between them and Us, and let an Impartial Judge determine where *Offence* may chiefly be taken, At our Solemn, Grave, and Serious Sett Forms, or their Wild Extempore⁵ Jargon, nauseaus to any Chaste or refin'd Ear. There are so many Absurdities committed by them, as wou'd shock one of our *Cherokee* Savages; And was a Sensible Turk or Indian to view some of their Extravagancies it would quickly determine them against Christianity. Had any such been in their Assembly as last Sunday when they communicated, the Honest Heathens would have imagin'd themselves rather amidst a Gang of frantic Lunatics broke out of Bedlam, rather than among a Society of religious Christians, met to celebrate the most sacred and Solemn Ordinance⁶ of their Religion. Here, one Fellow mounted on a Bench with the Bread, and bawling, *See the Body of Christ*, Another with the cup running around, and bellowing— *Who cleanses his Soul with the Blood of Christ*, and a thousand other Extravagancies—One on his knees in a Posture of Prayer—Others singing—some howling—These Ranting—Those Crying—Others dancing, Skipping, Laughing and rejoycing. Here two or 3 Women falling on their Backs, kicking up their Heels, exposing their Nakedness to all Bystanders and others sitting Pensive, in deep Melancholy lost in Abstraction, like Statues, quite insensible—and when rous'd by the Spectators from their pretended Reveries[,] Transports, and indecent Postures and Actions declaring they knew nought of the Matter. That their Souls had taken flight to Heav'n, and they knew nothing of what they said or did. Spect[at]ors were highly shocked at such vile Abuse of sacred Ordinances! And indeed such a Scene was sufficient to make the vilest Sinner shudder. Their Teacher, so far from condemning, or reproving, them, call'd it, the Work of God, and returned Thanks for Actions deserving of the Pillory and Whipping Post. But that would not have been *New* to some of them. And if they can thus transgress all bounds of Decency[,] Modesty, and Morality, in such an Open Public Manner, it is not hard to conceive what may pass at their Nocturnal Meetings, and Private Assemblies. Is there any thing like this in the Church of England to give Offence?

But another vile Matter that does and must give Offence to all Sober Minds Is, what they call their *Experiences*; It seems, that before

⁵Unplanned.
⁶The Lord's Supper, or Communion.

a Person be dipp'd,[7] He must give an Account of his Secret Calls, Conviction, Conversion, Repentance &c &c. Some of these Experiences have been so ludicrous and ridiculous that *Democritus*[8] in Spite of himself must have burst with Laughter. Others, altogether as blasphemous Such as their Visions, Dreams, Revelations—and the like; Too many, and too horrid to be mention'd. Nothing in the *Alcoran*[,][9] Nothing that can be found in all the Miracles of the Church of Rome, and all the Reveries of her Saints can be so absurd, or so Enthusiastic, as what has gravely been recited in that *Tabernacle* Yonder—To the Scandal of Religion and Insult of Common Sense. And to heighten the Farce, To see two or three fellows with fix'd Countenances and grave Looks, hearing all this Nonsense for Hours together, and making particular Enquiries, when, How, Where, in what Manner, these Miraculous Events happen'd—To see, I say, a Sett of Mongrels under Pretext of Religion, Sit, and hear for Hours together a String of Vile, cook'd up, Silly and Senseless Lyes, What they know to be Such, What they are Sensible has not the least foundation in Truth or Reason, and to encourage Persons in such Gross Inventions must grieve, must give great Offence to ev'ry one that has the Honour of Christianity at Heart.

[7]Baptized.
[8]An ancient Greek philosopher.
[9]The Qur'an, the holy book of Islam.

28

DANIEL FRISTOE

A Baptismal Service in Virginia

1771

Daniel Fristoe (1739–1774), a Baptist preacher, described in his diary an emotionally charged baptismal service, which apparently drew thousands of curious onlookers. Most churches in colonial America practiced infant baptism by sprinkling in indoor ceremonies. The Baptists caused a

From Lewis P. Little, *Imprisoned Preachers and Religious Liberty in Virginia* (Lynchburg, Va.: J. P. Bell and Co., 1938), 242–43.

sensation with their baptism of new converts by immersion in rivers or lakes. Many authorities did not welcome the Baptists' presence, and before the American Revolution, a number of Baptist itinerants were arrested, and sometimes beaten and fined, for illegal preaching in Virginia.

Satur. June 15

Met the brethren where I had been preaching for some time before in Foquire.[1] My first business was to examine candidates for baptism; as they were relating what God did for their souls one James Nayler came into the assembly and began to curse and swear and be very outrageous untill at last he blasphemed God and threw himself on the ground breaking the ground & tumbling like a fish taken out of the water untill at last one man for 10s[2] tied him and took him away; after which the congregation (which was very numerous) had peace; and 16 persons were adjudged proper subjects of baptism. The next day (being sunday) about 2000 people came together; after preaching, heard others that proposed to be baptized, 13 of which were deemed properly qualified. Then went to the water where I preached and baptized 29 persons. The trees about the water were so overloaded with spectators that some trees came down, but none hurt. The sight put me in mind of the story of Zackeus[3] and found afterwards that some came down to receive it. When I had finished we went to a field and making a circle in the center, there laid hands on the persons baptized. The multitude stood round weeping, but when we sang *Come we that love the lord*[4] & they were so affected that they lifted up their hands and faces towards heaven and discovered such chearful countenances in the midst of flowing tears as I had never seen before. In going away I looked back and saw multitudes, some roaring on the ground, some wringing their hands, some in extacies, some praying, some weeping; and other so outragious cursing & swearing that it was thought they were really possessed of the devil. I saw strange things today.

[1] Fauquier County, Virginia.
[2] Ten shillings.
[3] Luke 19. Zacchaeus climbed a tree to watch Jesus pass by.
[4] A hymn by the popular English hymn writer Isaac Watts.

29

MORGAN EDWARDS

A Public Baptism

1770

The drawing on page 126 shows Baptists baptizing adult converts in the Schuylkill River in Philadelphia. Such scenes also became common in the backcountry South during the two decades preceding the American Revolution. The drawing may help us imagine what Daniel Fristoe's baptismal service in Document 28 looked like.

Morgan Edwards, *Materials toward a History of the American Baptists* (Philadelphia, 1770), frontispiece.

SCHUYLKILL

6

Separatists, Baptists, and Religious Liberty

30

BOSTON GAZETTE

Church Separation in Canterbury, Connecticut

1742

Among the most outrageous actions of some radical evangelicals was breaking away from established churches and forming their own. Here an antagonistic newspaper correspondent reports on the uproar in Canterbury, Connecticut, after some radicals established their own unauthorized church. A lawyer, Elisha Paine (1693–1775), had been chosen as their minister despite his lack of formal training.

Canterbury is in worse confusion than ever. Their minister has left them, and they grow more noisy and boisterous so that they can get no minister to preach to them yet. Colonel Dyer exerted his authority among them on the Lord's Day, endeavoring to still them when many were exhorting and making a great hubbub, and ordered the constable to do his office, but they replied, "Get thee behind me, Satan!" and the noise and tumult Increased to such a degree, for above an hour, that the exhorter could not begin his exercise. Lawyer [Elisha] Paine has set up for a preacher . . . and makes it his business to go from house to house and town to town to gain proselytes to this new religion. Consequences are much feared.

From *Boston Gazette*, December 16, 1742, quoted in Ellen D. Larned, *History of Windham County, Connecticut* (Worcester, Mass., 1874), 1: 400.

31

A Letter from the Associated Ministers

1745

In 1745, the established ministers of Windham County, Connecticut, where the town of Canterbury is located, issued the statement against church separations excerpted here. Although these moderate evangelicals acknowledged that an authentic revival had occurred, they argued that the spirit behind the separations was satanic.

Dear Brethren and Friends:

We are well satisfied there has been of late, in a few Years past, a very great and merciful Revival of Religion in most of the Towns and Societies in this County, as well as in many other Places in this Land; which we desire to acknowledge to the Praise of Divine Grace: So we are fully satisfied there have been many Things which have accompanied this Work, which have really been of a different Kind. When it pleased GOD to send down the HOLY SPIRIT to convince and convert Sinners, and the Prince of Darkness was no longer able to keep them in that fatal Security and Formality in which they had lain, he was then obliged to act a different Part to carry on the Designs of his Kingdom of Darkness, and oppose the Conquests and Triumphs of the Redeemer. And this he has done by imitating, as nearly as he could, the Work of the HOLY GHOST, both by setting on imaginary Frights and Terrors, in some Instances, on Men's Minds, somewhat resembling the Conviction of the Blessed Spirit, and awakenings of Conscience for Sin; and also filling their Minds with Flashes of Joy, and false Comforts, resembling somewhat, in a general Way, the Consolations of the HOLY GHOST: In permitting which is to be adored the awful and mysterious Sovereignty of an holy GOD, *whose Way is in the Sea*, and *whose Footsteps are not known*.[1] This in its Beginning was not so plainly discerned and distinguished, in many Instances, from the Work of the HOLY SPIRIT, especially as there was sometimes some

---

[1]Psalm 77:19.

From *A Letter from the Associated Ministers of the County of Windham* (Boston, 1745), 3–6.

Mixture of such Things with the true Experiences of the People of
GOD; and it was also partly owing to the injudicious and violent Opposition of some to this Work; who, while they saw bad Things attending
it, and many People taken with them, boldly concluded, it was all of a
Piece, and with tremendous Rashness ascribed it all to the Devil:
While others, on the other Hand, looking on the Good, and being persuaded that it was a Day of GOD's wonderful Power, and gracious Visitation, suddenly and weakly concluded, that there was little Wrong in
the Appearances, besides mere human Weaknesses, and unavoidable
Infirmity: This gave great advantage to the subtle Powers of Darkness
to sow Tares in the Field, and execute their wicked Designs, which
now more and more appear to have been to raise Men's Tempers,
throw them into Parties; to excite and keep up a blind and furious
Zeal, and embitter their Spirits, and set them on to reproach and per-
secute one another; to lead off their Minds from the true and proper
Concerns of Religion; to deceive some with false Shows of Zeal for the
Cause of GOD; to lead many into wrong and false Notions of the
Nature of Regeneration, and lead off their Minds from the Word of
GOD; to puff them up with Pride and vain Notions of immediate
Impulses on their Minds, and Apprehensions of being taught their
Duty, and the doctrinal Meaning of particular Texts of Scripture
thereby; to lead them off from the Ordinances of CHRIST, and persuade them of the Uselessness of the ordinary Means of Teaching,
and render them deaf to all Conviction, but what they think is from
the Spirit of GOD speaking in them; and also to prejudice the Minds
of carnal and inexperienced Persons against the Doctrine of Regeneration and the Necessity of a special Work of the Holy Spirit to convince
and renew them; to satisfy themselves without any such Work, and to
think that all that is beyond mere outward Morality and Virtue and
what Reformation is wrought by mere moral Swasion, is nothing but
wild Rant, Superstition and Folly, and the Issue of these Things is
Deism and Infidelity. As these Designs of the grand Adversary have
opened more, and we have great Reason to fear that many Persons, in
several of the Places we have the esp[e]cial Charge of, have been suffered by GOD's righteous Judgment to be deceived, and have run into
such Errors and Miscarriages, as evidently to become the Instruments of Satan to carry on some of these Designs and Occasions of
stirring up others to such severe Treatment of them, as hardens them
more and more in their Errors, and many are drawn away after them,
partly out of pity to them, and by wrong Conclusions, that their Sufferings are an Evidence that they are right, and partly out of Opposition

to others whom they think to be carnal and ungodly Men: We have in our respective Places, as GOD has enabled us, endeavoured to convince and recover them, and help them to discern the Snares of the Devil, but since private Endeavours have proved insufficient, we have lately united to give our publick Testimony against some Things, which we dare no longer forbear openly to testify against; and therein told you that we purposed by GOD's help more particularly to do it in a little Time: And the rather, as you well know there are diverse Persons in several of our Societies, who have of late separated themselves from the Congregations to which they did belong, and have vented diverse erroneous and dangerous Principles, calculated to overthrow the Institution of the Gospel Ministry; to render vain the Ordinances of CHRIST's Appointment; to the perverting of the holy Scriptures, and making some of the great and most important Doctrines of the holy Scriptures, appear in a ridiculous Light, and have followed several Persons who have set up for publick Teachers and Exhorters (as far as we can find on the same Principles) and draw away the People after them, to the Neglect and Contempt of the instituted Worship of GOD.

Some of the most considerable of these Errors are these that follow;

1. That it is the Will of GOD to have a pure Church on Earth, in this Sense, that all the Converted should be separated from the Unconverted.

2. That the Saints certainly know one another, and know who are CHRIST's true Ministers, by their own inward Feelings, or a Communion between them in the inward Actings of their own Souls.

3. That no other Call is necessary to a Person's Undertaking to preach the Gospel, but his being a true Christian, and having an inward Motion of the Spirit, or a Perswasion in his own Mind that it is the Will of GOD he should preach and perform ministerial Acts: The Consequence of which is, that there is no standing instituted Ministry in the Christian Church which may be known by the visible Laws of CHRIST's Kingdom.

4. That GOD disowns the Ministry and Churches in this Land, and the Ordinances as administered in them.

5. That at such Meetings of Lay-preaching and Exhorting they have more of the Presence of GOD, than in His Ordinances, and under the Ministration of the present Ministry, and Administration of the Ordinances [i]n these Churches. And hereupon many Persons

have chosen to follow after such as have set up themselves to be
Preachers, Exhorters and Expounders of the Doctrines of the Scriptures; several of which there have sprung up of late in this County, the
most famous of which is Mr. *Elisha Paine*, of whose Mistakes and
Errors in these Points, we have had diverse Informations, and some of
us have taken Pains to recover him, and others who practice in like
manner, though to no purpose: But as the People's Errors and wild
Zeal increase, so the Admiration of these Teachers increases, so that
they are often crying, *Never Man spoke like these Men*, at least, crying
them up above all their Teachers. Now as to our own Parts, we hope
we could be content to have our Names sink and be despised, if
CHRIST was but honoured, and the Souls of his People edified; but
being sufficiently convinced of the contrary, and that our blessed Saviour, the LORD JESUS, is abused, and his Name reproached under a
show of great Zeal and Love to it, his Laws broken, his Word per-
verted and his Ordinances despised, under a pretence of advancing
his Glory; the People in danger of being led into still more fatal
Errors; and yet all to promote their Salvation: We could not answer it
to our divine LORD, nor to your Souls, any longer to forbear giving our
most open Testimony against these Things.

32

SOLOMON PAINE

Petition for Religious Liberty

1748

*Solomon Paine (1698–1754), brother of Elisha, became the pastor of the
separatist church in Canterbury in 1746. In the petition excerpted here,
which 330 people signed, Paine requested that the Connecticut assembly
repeal punishments and taxes against religious dissenters and separatists, but the appeal was denied.*

From Solomon Paine, *A Short View of the Difference* (Newport, R.I., 1752), 8–11.

That whereas the living and true God in his Holy Word, hath commanded all Men to fear God and honour the King,[1] and that their Fear
towards God ought to be taught by his unerring Word, and not by the
Precepts of Men; and hath given to every Man an unalienable Right
in Matters of the Worship of God, to judge for himself, as his Conscience receives the Rule from God, who alone hath Right to challenge Sovereignty over, and Propriety in them: And he hath showed
the Zeal he hath for his own Worship, both by Threatenings, and
inflicting heavy Judgments upon those who dare to usurp this Authority over the Consciences of others, and teach for Doctrine the Commandments of Men; and also in promising to, and conferring great
Favours upon those who have appeared uprightly to stand for the
Glory of God, in Liberty of Conscience in all Ages, and particularly
upon our Fore-Fathers, who left their Native Country for an howling
Wilderness, full of savage Men and Beasts, that they might have Liberty of Conscience. . . .

And whereas, your Honours' Memorialists, and many more of their
Neighbours, who worship with them in the Fear of God, cannot without doing Violence to their own Consciences, profess to be of any of
the abovesaid Churches, or of their Way of Worship, and so neglect to
worship God according to their own Consciences, as they understand
the Word of God by his Holy Spirit. But since the Grace of God hath
appeared to them, teaching them to deny all Ungodliness, & etc. they
are determined, by Divine Assistance, to obey God, and worship him
in Spirit and in Truth, although that Way be called *Independent* or *Separate*, and to honour the King as supreme, and Governors as sent by
him, in yielding Obedience to them in all civil Matters.

And yet they are all exposed, either to make Shipwreck of a good
Conscience, or to suffer by Fines or Imprisonment, as many of them
have already suffered, for preaching the Gospel, and other Acts of
Divine Service, in Obedience to the Commands, and by the Power of
God's Spirit; and great Quantities of their temporal Goods, with which
they should serve God and honour the King, are taken from them to
support that Worship which they cannot in Conscience uphold: And
they knowing that the doing such Violence endangers Souls, and also
Common-wealths, and is threatened in the Word of God, with public
Calamity, or eternal Punishment, he shall have Judgment without
Mercy, that hath showed no Mercy, and Mercy rejoiceth against Judg-

[1] 1 Peter 2:17.

ment, for they shall be judged by the Law of Liberty. And seeing the Judgments of Almighty God are coming upon this Land, and the abovesaid Imposition and Oppression still carried on: Whereupon your Honours' Memorialists pray, That your Honours may be the happy Instruments of unbinding these Burdens, and enact universal Liberty, by repealing all those Ecclesiastical Laws that are or may be executed to the debarring[2] of any of this Colony of the Liberty granted by God, and tolerated by our King; or forbid the Execution of said Laws: And they, as in Duty bound, shall ever pray.

[2]Denying.

33

ISAAC BACKUS

Reasons for Separation

1756

Isaac Backus (1724–1806) of Norwich, Connecticut, also participated in an illegal church separation in the 1740s. In the document excerpted here, written ten years later, he gave the reasons that he believed justified such a separation. Many radical evangelicals such as Backus desired what they called a "pure" church, with only converted believers allowed into membership.

1. When manifest unbelivers are indulged in the Church, Gods people are called to seperate from 'em, 2 Corinthians 6:14–17. Should any object that this intends to seperate from Heathen idolitors, I reply that unrighteous heathens are no worse than those who make their boast of the law and yet thro' breaking of it dishonor God, Romans 2:23 etc. And how much better is he that makes a God of his belly or of his money than those who set up a Carved image, Philippians 3:19;

From Isaac Backus, "Reasons of Separation," in *The Diary of Isaac Backus*, ed. William G. McLoughlin (Providence, R.I.: Brown University Press, 1979), 3: 1527–28.

REV·ISAAC BACKUS·AM·

Figure 5. *Isaac Backus, Andover Newton Theological School, no date.*
Converted in Connecticut during the First Great Awakening in the early
1740s, Backus became attracted to evangelical radicalism, first in the
separatist movement and then among the Baptists. He became the most
articulate opponent of church establishments in Revolutionary era New
England.

Franklin Trask Library, Andover Newton Theological School.

134

Ephesians 5:5. Those who can frame their religion to suit worldly gain we are required to withdraw from, 1 Timothy 6:5.

2. When the Clear doctrines of Christ are not preacht but Godsword is corrupted Such messengers are to be avoided, 2 John 10:11. We are Commanded to Cease from hearing the instructions that cause us to err from the ways of Knowledge, Proverbs 19:27.

3. When the clear gospel and messengers of Christ are shut out we are to go without the Camp bearing his reproach, Hebrews 33:13. When the Church of the Jews at E[p]hesus were hardened against the gospel Paul withdrew and seperated the disciples, Acts 19:9 and 13:46 etc.

4. Those that have the form of Godliness but [deny] the power thereof we are to turn away from, 2 Timothy 3:5. By the form of Godliness I understand [the] profession of knowing and conforming to Gods law, Romans 2:2. The power of it is that whereby Souls are deliverd from the power of sin and Satan and are brought to live to God by faith, Romans 1:16–17. And those deny it who can admit persons into the Church without sufficient evidence that they have experienced it, and so do all those who don't live such a life. Such profess that they know God but in Works deny him, Titus 1:16.

34

ISAAC BACKUS

Conversion to Baptist Principles

1751

Many separatists in New England became convinced that the Congregational Church's practice of infant baptism was unbiblical. Backus, who had become a separatist minister in Titicut, Massachusetts (near present-day Bridgewater), started to believe in adult, or believer's, baptism by

From William G. McLoughlin, ed., *The Diary of Isaac Backus* (Providence, R.I.: Brown University Press, 1979), 1:143, 147–48.

immersion, which he received in 1751. He described his conversion to these principles in his diary.

At a Church meeting Thursday July 25, 1751 I told the Church that I was more fully Convinced That there wasn't Scripture grounds for Infant Baptism which heretofore we had gone on in and we had some discourse upon It. And we agreed to Send to the Churches in Norwich, in Canterbury, Plainfield, Providence, And Cambridge norwest Parish to come to give us advice in our present Case on Sept. 4th Next ensuing. . . .

Thursday Aug. 22
Brother Benjamin Pierce Pastor of a Church in part of Warwick Preached among us at Brother Hindses this Day with Considerable Power; and then in the Afternoon Concluded to Baptize Some Persons. Now in the morning I had Thoughts of going to a meeting at Norton Today but Providence Seemed to shut up The way; So I went to this meeting: and tho' I felt dreadful Struggles in my mind About many things in the morning—Yet I had Sweet Refreshings under his preaching. And when I Came to see him Baptize Sundry persons, I having been convinced before that the Way that I used to go on in, In Baptizing Infants and by Sprinkling was not according to Scripture—and having this opportunity to Practice as I now believed Was right—I [dared not] put it off. Therefore I told Some account of my Conversion and Then of my experiences as to these Things, which gave Satisfaction; then I went down Into the Water with him And was Baptized. And both then and Afterwards in the evening I felt a sweet Calmness of mind and some things opened with Special clearness to my Soul. Blessed be God.

35

ISAAC BACKUS

An Appeal to the Public for Religious Liberty

1773

*Along with Solomon Paine, Backus became one of early America's fore-
most defenders of religious liberty, as separatists and Baptists both faced
punishments for their dissenting practices and had to pay taxes to support the established churches of New England. In this treatise, Backus
contended that just as Americans sought their liberty against the unjust
taxes of Great Britain (the Declaration of Independence was just three
years away), so also the Baptists needed relief from the oppression of the
colonial governments. Backus took the lead in arguing that no one
should be punished by the state for his or her religious views.*

And now our dear countrymen, we beseech you seriously to consider
of these things. The great importance of a general union through this
country, in order to the preservation of our liberties, has often been
pleaded for with propriety; but how can such a union be expected so
long as that dearest of all rights, equal liberty of conscience is not
allowed? Yea, how can any reasonably expect that HE who has the
hearts of kings in his hand, will turn the heart of our earthly sovereign to hear the pleas for liberty, of those who will not hear the cries
of their fellow-subjects, under their oppressions? Has it not been
plainly proved, that so far as any man gratifies his own inclinations,
without regard to the universal law of equity, so far he is in bondage?
So that it is impossible for any one to tyrannize over others, without
thereby becoming a miserable slave himself: a slave to raging lusts,
and a slave to guilty fears of what will be the consequence. . . .

Suffer us a little to expostulate with our fathers and brethren, who
inhabit the land to which our ancestors fled for religious liberty. You
have lately been accused with being disorderly and rebellious, by men
in power, who profess a great regard for order and the public good;

From Isaac Backus, *An Appeal to the Public for Religious Liberty* (Boston, 1773), 52–59.

and why don't you believe them, and rest easy under their administrations? You tell us you cannot, because you are taxed where you are not represented; and is it not really so with us? You do not deny the right of the British parliament to impose taxes within her own realm; only complain that she extends her taxing power beyond her proper limits; and have we not as good right to say you do the *same thing*? and so that wherein you judge others you condemn yourselves? Can three thousand miles possibly fix such limits to taxing power, as the difference between civil and sacred matters has already done? One is only a distance of *space*, the other is so great a difference in the *nature* of things, as there is between *sacrifices to God*, and the *ordinances of men*. . . .

Many think it hard to be frowned upon only for pleading for their rights, and laying open particular acts of encroachment thereon; but what frowns have we met with for no other crime? and as the present contest between Great-Britain and America, is not so much about the greatness of the taxes already laid, as about a submission to their taxing power; so (though what we have already suffered is far from being a trifle, yet) our greatest difficulty at present concerns the submitting to a taxing power in ecclesiastical affairs. It is supposed by many that we are exempted from such taxes, but they are greatly mistaken, for all knew that paper is a money article, and writing upon it is labour, and this tax we must pay every year, as a token of submission to their power, or else they will lay a heavier tax upon us. And we have one difficulty in submitting to this power, which our countrymen have not in the other case: that is, our case affects the conscience, as theirs does not: and equal liberty of conscience is one essential article in our CHARTER, which constitutes this government, and describes the extent of our rulers authority, and what are the rights and liberties of the people. And in the confession of faith[1] which our rulers and their ministers have published to the world, they say, "God alone is Lord of the conscience, and hath left it free from the doctrines and commandments of men, which are, in *any thing* contrary to his word; or *not contained in it*; so that to believe such doctrines, or to obey such commands, out of conscience, is to *betray* true liberty of conscience; and the requiring of an implicit faith, and an absolute blind obedience, is to destroy liberty of conscience and reason also." . . .

[1]The Westminster Confession of Faith (1646), a commonly used statement of Calvinist doctrine.

If the constitution of this government, gives the magistrate no other authority than what belongs to *civil society*, we desire to know how he ever came to *impose* any particular *way of worship*, upon any town or precinct whatsoever? And if a man has a right to his *estate*, his *liberty* and his *family*, notwithstanding his non-conformity to the magistrates way of worship, by what authority has any man had his goods spoiled, his land sold, or his person imprisoned, and thereby deprived of the enjoyment both of his liberty and his family, for no crime at all against the peace or welfare of the state, but only because he refused to conform to, or to support an *imposed* way of worship, or an *imposed* minister.

In a celebrated oration for liberty, published last spring in Boston, a maxim was recited which carries it's own evidence with it, which is this, NO MAN CAN GIVE THAT WHICH IS ANOTHER'S. Yet have not our legislature from time to time, made acts to empower the major part of the inhabitants in towns and precincts, to *give away* their neighbors estates to what ministers they please! And can we submit to such doctrines and commandments of men, and not *betray* true liberty of conscience!

36

JOHN LELAND

The Rights of Conscience Inalienable

1791

John Leland (1754–1841), a Baptist minister in Virginia and New England, helped lead the effort for disestablishment in Virginia, Connecticut, and Massachusetts. Although Leland and non-evangelicals such as Thomas Jefferson and James Madison held very different religious beliefs, they cooperated to disestablish the Anglican Church in Virginia in 1786. Baptists such as Leland knew intimately the dangers of government persecution for unpopular religious views, as many Baptist itinerants had

From John Leland, *The Rights of Conscience Inalienable* (New London, Conn., 1791), 7, 13–14.

been punished in Virginia in the 1770s. In the document excerpted here, Leland expressed a view very similar to Jefferson's that government should not give preference to any religious group, but should protect the rights of religious minorities to express their views and practice their beliefs in safety.

1. Every man must give an account of himself to God, and therefore every man ought to be at liberty to serve God in that way that he can best reconcile it to his conscience. If Government can answer for Individuals at the day of judgement, let men be controlled by it, in religious matters; otherwise, let men be free.

2. It would be sinful for a man to surrender that to man, which is to be kept sacred for God. A man's mind should always be open to conviction; and an honest man will receive that doctrine which appears the best demonstrated: and what is more common than for the best of men to change their minds? . . .

Is uniformity of sentiments, in matters of religion, essential to the happiness of civil government? Not at all. Government has no more to do with the religious opinions of men, than it has with the principles of the mathematicks. Let every man speak freely without fear — maintain the principles that he believes — worship according to his own faith, either one God, three Gods, no God, or twenty Gods; and let government protect him in so doing, i.e. see that he meets with no personal abuse or loss of property, for his religious opinions. Instead of discouraging of him with proscriptions, fines, confiscation or death, let him be encouraged, as a free man, to bring forth his arguments and maintain his points with all boldness: then, if his doctrine is false, it will be confuted, and if it is true (though ever so novel) let others credit it.

When every man has liberty, what can he wish for more? A liberal man asks for nothing more of government.

A Chronology of the Great Awakening (1727–1791)

1727 An earthquake causes a significant revival in New England.

1734–
1735 A revival breaks out in Jonathan Edwards's Northampton, Massachusetts, congregation.

1735 George Whitefield is converted at Oxford University.

1737 Edwards's *A Faithful Narrative* is published.

1738 Whitefield visits America for the first time and decides to start an orphanage in Georgia.

1739 Timothy Cutler writes a letter critiquing the Northampton revival.

1739–
1741 Whitefield visits America for the second time and sees his greatest evangelistic successes there.

1740 A revival begins in Samuel Blair's church in New Londonderry, Pennsylvania.

Gilbert Tennent delivers *The Danger of an Unconverted Ministry*.

Josiah Smith publishes *The Character, Preaching, &c. of the Rev. Mr. George Whitefield*.

Samson Occom is converted in Connecticut.

1741 Jonathan Edwards preaches "Sinners in the Hands of an Angry God" in Enfield, Connecticut.

Edwards delivers *The Distinguishing Marks* at the Yale commencement.

1742 Hugh Bryan is arrested in South Carolina for fomenting rebellion among the slaves.

James Davenport is arrested and deported from Connecticut, then arrested and declared insane in Boston.

A.M. publishes *The State of Religion in New England* in Glasgow.

1743 Davenport holds a book and clothes burning in New London, Connecticut.

Edwards publishes *Some Thoughts concerning the Present Revival of Religion in New England*, and Charles Chauncy counters with *Seasonable Thoughts on the State of Religion in New England*.

Mercy Wheeler is healed in Plainfield, Connecticut.

Moderate Boston ministers issue *The Testimony and Advice of an Assembly of Pastors*.

1744 Davenport publishes his *Confession and Retractions*.

1745 The Yale College faculty publishes *The Declaration of the Rector and Tutors* denouncing Whitefield.

Isaac Backus and others separate from the established church in Norwich, Connecticut.

1748 Solomon Paine and Connecticut separatists submit an appeal for religious liberty but are denied.

Samuel Davies becomes the minister of Hanover County, Virginia's Presbyterian congregations.

1751 Backus converts to Baptist principles and receives believer's baptism.

1754 The Seven Years' War begins in America, where it is known as the French and Indian War.

1755 Shubal Stearns and Daniel Marshall form the Sandy Creek Baptist Church in North Carolina.

1757 Samuel Davies publishes *Letters from the Rev. Samuel Davies* in London; describes the faith of some African American slaves in his congregation.

1763 The Seven Years' War ends.

1764 Samuel Buell's Easthampton, Long Island, congregation experiences a revival.

1765 The Stamp Act crisis begins in the American colonies.

1770 John Marrant is converted in Charleston, South Carolina.

Whitefield dies in Newburyport, Massachusetts.

1771 Daniel Fristoe describes an outdoor baptismal service in Virginia.

1773 Backus publishes *An Appeal to the Public for Religious Liberty*.

1775 The Battles of Lexington and Concord begin the American Revolution.

1783 The Treaty of Paris ends the American Revolution.

1786 The Act Establishing Religious Freedom is passed in Virginia.

1789   The U.S. Constitution is ratified.

1791   The Bill of Rights is adopted, including the First Amendment, its "free exercise" of religion clause, and prohibition of an "establishment of religion" by the federal government.

John Leland publishes *The Rights of Conscience Inalienable.*

Questions for Consideration

1. Why were evangelicals such as Jonathan Edwards, George Whitefield, and Gilbert Tennent so consumed with the idea of the "new birth"?
2. How do Jonathan Edwards's and Timothy Cutler's interpretations of the Northampton awakening differ?
3. Why was Whitefield such a popular preacher?
4. Why did so many people in America, such as Stephen Bordley and the faculty of Yale College, dislike the effects of Whitefield's preaching?
5. Why did evangelical faith appeal to people such as Nathan Cole, Samson Occom, Mercy Wheeler, and John Marrant?
6. Why did revivals and meetings such as those described by Daniel Rogers, Samuel Buell, and Daniel Fristoe generate such powerful emotions? How did those emotions lead to criticism of the revivalists?
7. Historians have a hard time evaluating dramatic spiritual episodes such as prophecies, visions, and healings. How should we evaluate these sorts of experiences as described in the documents by Daniel Rogers, the anonymous visionary, and Mercy Wheeler (see Documents 12, 13, and 14)?
8. What were James Davenport's motivations? Was he insane, as declared by the Boston court?
9. According to Jonathan Edwards, what was the best way to evaluate the legitimacy of a revival?
10. What practices seen in the First Great Awakening were especially disruptive or offensive?
11. What challenges did evangelicals face in the South because of the predominance of slavery? What effect did evangelicalism have on southern whites and on southern African Americans?
12. How would you compare the racial views of George Whitefield, Hugh Bryan, and Samuel Davies?
13. Why did people such as A.M. and Charles Woodmason see evangelicals as such a big threat?

144

14. Why were church separations seen as such a grievous problem in New England? What motivated those who separated?

15. How would you describe Solomon Paine's, Isaac Backus's, and John Leland's views of the relationship between church and state? How do these early separatists' and Baptists' appeals compare with modern American ideas about church-state relations?

16. How would you define the First Great Awakening?

17. Why did the Great Awakening happen?

18. How did the Great Awakening change American religion and society?

19. To what extent would you describe the Great Awakening as having radical effects or implications?

20. What is the significance of the Great Awakening in American history?

Selected Bibliography

GENERAL

Bonomi, Patricia. *Under the Cope of Heaven: Religion, Society, and Politics in Colonial America.* New York: Oxford University Press, 1986.

Brockway, Robert W. *A Wonderful Work of God: Puritanism and the Great Awakening.* Bethlehem, Pa.: Lehigh University Press, 2003.

Bumsted, J. M., and John E. van de Wetering. *What Must I Do to Be Saved? The Great Awakening in Colonial America.* Hinsdale, Ill.: Dryden Press, 1976.

Butler, Jon. *Awash in a Sea of Faith: Christianizing the American People.* Cambridge, Mass.: Harvard University Press, 1990.

———. "Enthusiasm Described and Decried: The Great Awakening as Interpretative Fiction." *Journal of American History,* 69, no. 2 (September, 1982): 305–25.

Cowing, Cedric B. *The Great Awakening and the American Revolution: Colonial Thought in the 18th Century.* Chicago: Rand McNally, 1971.

Hall, Timothy. *Contested Boundaries: Itinerancy and the Reshaping of the Colonial American Religious World.* Durham, N.C.: Duke University Press, 1994.

Hempton, David. *Methodism: Empire of the Spirit.* New Haven, Conn.: Yale University Press, 2005.

Lambert, Frank. *Inventing the "Great Awakening."* Princeton, N.J.: Princeton University Press, 1999.

———. *"Pedlar in Divinity": George Whitefield and the Transatlantic Revivals, 1737–1770.* Princeton, N.J.: Princeton University Press, 1994.

Noll, Mark A. *America's God: From Jonathan Edwards to Abraham Lincoln.* New York: Oxford University Press, 2002.

———. *The Rise of Evangelicalism: The Age of Edwards, Whitefield and the Wesleys.* Downers Grove, Ill.: InterVarsity Press, 2003.

O'Brien, Susan. "A Transatlantic Community of Saints: The Great Awakening and the First Evangelical Network, 1735–1755." *American Historical Review,* 91, no. 4 (October 1986): 811–32.

Stout, Harry S. *The Divine Dramatist: George Whitefield and the Rise of Modern Evangelicalism.* Grand Rapids, Mich.: Eerdmans, 1991.

Tracy, Joseph. *The Great Awakening: A History of the Revival of Religion in the Time of Edwards and Whitefield*. Carlisle, Pa.: Banner of Truth, 1976, Reprint of 1842 edition.

Ward, W. R. *The Protestant Evangelical Awakening*. New York: Cambridge University Press, 1992.

NEW ENGLAND

Breen, T. H., and Timothy Hall. "Structuring Provincial Imagination: The Rhetoric and Experience of Social Change in Eighteenth-Century New England." *American Historical Review*, 103, no. 5 (1998): 1411–39.

Bushman, Richard L. *From Puritan to Yankee: Character and the Social Order in Connecticut, 1690–1765*. Cambridge, Mass.: Harvard University Press, 1967.

Cooper, James F., Jr. *Tenacious of Their Liberties: The Congregationalists in Colonial Massachusetts*. New York: Oxford University Press, 1999.

Crawford, Michael J. *Seasons of Grace: Colonial New England's Revival Tradition in Its British Context*. New York: Oxford University Press, 1991.

Davidson, James W. *The Logic of Millennial Thought: Eighteenth-Century New England*. New Haven, Conn.: Yale University Press, 1977.

Gaustad, Edwin S. *The Great Awakening in New England*. New York: Harper and Row, 1957.

Grasso, Christopher. *A Speaking Aristocracy: Transforming Public Discourse in Eighteenth-Century Connecticut*. Chapel Hill: University of North Carolina Press, 1999.

Griffin, Edward M. *Old Brick: Charles Chauncy of Boston, 1705–1787*. Minneapolis: University of Minnesota Press, 1980.

Gura, Philip F. *Jonathan Edwards: America's Evangelical*. New York: Hill and Wang, 2005.

Harlan, David. *The Clergy and the Great Awakening in New England*. Ann Arbor, Mich.: UMI Research Press, 1979.

Kidd, Thomas S. *The Protestant Interest: New England after Puritanism*. New Haven, Conn.: Yale University Press, 2004.

Lippy, Charles H. *Seasonable Revolutionary: The Mind of Charles Chauncy*. Chicago: Nelson-Hall, 1981.

Marsden, George M. *Jonathan Edwards: A Life*. New Haven, Conn.: Yale University Press, 2003.

McLoughlin, William G. *Isaac Backus and the American Pietistic Tradition*. Boston: Little, Brown, 1967.

Olivas, J. Richard. "Partial Revival: The Limits of the Great Awakening in Boston, Massachusetts, 1740–1742." In *Inequality in Early America*, edited by Carla G. Pestana and Sharon V. Salinger, 67–86. Dartmouth, N.H.: University Press of New England, 1999.

148

SELECTED BIBLIOGRAPHY

Seeman, Erik. *Pious Persuasions: Laity and Clergy in Eighteenth-Century New England.* Baltimore: Johns Hopkins University Press, 1999.
Stout, Harry S. *The New England Soul: Preaching and Religious Culture in Colonial New England.* New York: Oxford University Press, 1986.

MIDDLE COLONIES

Coalter, Milton J. Jr. *Gilbert Tennent, Son of Thunder: A Case Study of Continental Pietism's Impact on the First Great Awakening in the Middle Colonies.* Westport, Conn.: Greenwood Press, 1986.
Griffin, Patrick. *The People with No Name: Ireland's Ulster Scots, America's Scots Irish, and the Creation of a British Atlantic World, 1689–1764.* Princeton, N.J.: Princeton University Press, 2001.
Landsman, Ned. *Scotland and Its First American Colony, 1683–1765.* Princeton, N.J.: Princeton University Press, 1985.
Le Beau, Bryan F. *Jonathan Dickinson and the Formative Years of American Presbyterianism.* Lexington: University Press of Kentucky, 1997.
Maxson, Charles H. *The Great Awakening in the Middle Colonies.* Chicago: University of Chicago Press, 1920.
Schmidt, Leigh Eric. *Holy Fairs: Scotland and the Making of American Revivalism,* 2nd ed. Grand Rapids, Mich.: Eerdmans, 2001.
Westerkamp, Marilyn J. *The Triumph of the Laity: Scots-Irish Piety and the Great Awakening, 1625–1760.* New York: Oxford University Press, 1988.

SOUTHERN COLONIES

Calhoon, Robert M. *Evangelicals and Conservatives in the Early South, 1740–1861.* Columbia: University of South Carolina Press, 1988.
Gewehr, Wesley M. *The Great Awakening in Virginia, 1740–1790.* Durham, N.C.: Duke University Press, 1930.
Isaac, Rhys. *The Transformation of Virginia, 1740–1790.* Chapel Hill: University of North Carolina Press, 1982.
Jackson, Harvey H. "Hugh Bryan and the Evangelical Movement in Colonial South Carolina." *William and Mary Quarterly,* 3rd ser., 43, no. 4 (October 1986): 594–614.
Kidd, Thomas S. "'A Faithful Watchman on the Walls of Charlestown': Josiah Smith and Moderate Revivalism in Colonial South Carolina." *South Carolina Historical Magazine,* 105, no. 2 (April 2004): 82–106.
Lindman, Janet Moore. "Acting the Manly Christian: White Evangelical Masculinity in Revolutionary Virginia." *William and Mary Quarterly,* 3rd ser., 57, no. 2 (April 2000): 393–416.
Little, Thomas J. "'Adding to the Church Such as Shall be Saved': The Growth in Influence of Evangelicalism in Colonial South Carolina, 1740–1775." In *Money, Trade, and Power: The Evolution of Colonial South Carolina's Plantation Society,* edited by Jack P. Greene, Rose-

mary Brana-Shute, and Randy J. Sparks. Columbia: University of South Carolina Press, 2001: 363–82.

AFRICAN AMERICANS, NATIVE AMERICANS, AND THE GREAT AWAKENING

Brooks, Joanna. *American Lazarus: Religion and the Rise of African-American and Native American Literatures.* New York: Oxford University Press, 2003.

Brooks, Joanna, and John Saillant, eds. *"Face Zion Forward": First Writers of the Black Atlantic, 1785–1798.* Boston: Northeastern University Press, 2002.

Frey, Sylvia R., and Betty Wood. *Come Shouting to Zion: African American Protestantism in the American South and British Caribbean to 1830.* Chapel Hill: University of North Carolina Press, 1998.

Love, William DeLoss. *Samson Occom and the Christian Indians of New England.* Syracuse, N.Y.: Syracuse University Press, 2000. Reprint of 1899 edition with introduction by Margaret C. Szasz.

Merritt, Jane T. "Dreaming of the Saviour's Blood: Moravians and the Indian Great Awakening in Pennsylvania." *William and Mary Quarterly,* 3rd ser., 54, no. 4 (October 1997): 723–46.

Seeman, Erik. "'Justise Must Take Plase': Three African Americans Speak of Religion in Eighteenth-Century New England." *William and Mary Quarterly,* 3rd ser., 56, no. 2 (April 1999): 393–414.

Sobel, Mechal. *Trabelin' On: The Slave Journey to an Afro-Baptist Faith.* Paperback ed. Princeton, N.J.: Princeton University Press, 1988.

WOMEN AND THE GREAT AWAKENING

Brekus, Catherine A. *Strangers and Pilgrims: Female Preaching in America, 1740–1845.* Chapel Hill: University of North Carolina Press, 1998.

Hambrick-Stowe, Charles E. "The Spiritual Pilgrimage of Sarah Osborn (1714–1796)." *Church History,* 61, no. 4 (December 1992): 408–21.

Kidd, Thomas S. "The Healing of Mercy Wheeler: Illness and Miracles among Early American Evangelicals." *William and Mary Quarterly,* 3rd ser., 63, no. 1 (January 2006): 149–70.

Juster, Susan. *Disorderly Women: Sexual Politics and Evangelicalism in Revolutionary New England.* Ithaca, N.Y.: Cornell University Press, 1994.

Lacey, Barbara E., ed. *The World of Hannah Heaton: The Diary of an Eighteenth-Century Connecticut Farm Woman.* De Kalb: Northern Illinois University Press, 2003.

EVANGELICAL RADICALISM

Cray, Robert E., Jr. "More Light on a New Light: James Davenport's Religious Legacy, Eastern Long Island, 1740–1840." *New York History,* 73, no. 1 (1992): 5–27.

Goen, C. C. *Revivalism and Separatism in New England, 1740–1800: Strict Congregationalists and Separate Baptists in the Great Awakening.* Rev. ed. Middletown, Conn.: Wesleyan University Press, 1987.

Marini, Stephen A. *Radical Sects of Revolutionary New England.* Cambridge, Mass.: Harvard University Press, 1982.

Rawlyk, George A. *The Canada Fire: Radical Evangelicalism in British North America, 1775–1812.* Kingston, Ont.: McGill-Queen's University Press, 1994.

Schmidt, Leigh Eric. "'A Second and Glorious Reformation': The New Light Extremism of Andrew Croswell." *William and Mary Quarterly,* 3rd ser., 43, no. 2 (April 1986): 214-44.

Sparks, Elder John. *The Roots of Appalachian Christianity: The Life and Legacy of Elder Shubal Stearns.* Lexington: University Press of Kentucky, 2001.

Stout, Harry S., and Peter Onuf. "James Davenport and the Great Awakening in New London." *Journal of American History,* 70, no. 3 (December 1983): 556-78.

Taves, Ann. *Fits, Trances, and Visions: Experiencing Religion and Explaining Experience from Wesley to James.* Princeton, N.J.: Princeton University Press, 1999.

Winiarski, Douglas L. "Jonathan Edwards, Enthusiast? Radical Revivalism and the Great Awakening in the Connecticut Valley." *Church History,* 74, no. 4 (December 2005): 683-739.

————. "Souls Filled with Ravishing Transport: Heavenly Visions and the Radical Awakening in New England." *William and Mary Quarterly,* 3rd ser., 61, no. 1 (January 2004): 3-46.

RELIGION AND THE AMERICAN REVOLUTION

Bloch, Ruth. *Visionary Republic: Millennial Themes in American Thought, 1756–1800.* New York: Cambridge University Press, 1985.

Goff, Philip. "Revivals and Revolution: Historiographic Turns since Alan Heimert's *Religion and the American Mind.*" *Church History,* 67, no. 4 (December 1998): 695-721.

Hatch, Nathan O. *The Sacred Cause of Liberty: Republican Thought and the Millennium in Revolutionary New England.* New Haven, Conn.: Yale University Press, 1977.

Heimert, Alan. *Religion and the American Mind: From the Great Awakening to the Revolution.* Cambridge, Mass.: Harvard University Press, 1966.

Hoffman, Ronald, and Peter J. Albert, eds. *Religion in a Revolutionary Age.* Charlottesville: University Press of Virginia, 1994.

Noll, Mark A. *Christians in the American Revolution.* Vancouver, B.C.: Regent College Publishing, 2006. Reprint of 1977 edition.

Stout, Harry S. "Religion, Communications, and the Ideological Origins of the American Revolution." *William and Mary Quarterly,* 3rd ser., 34, no. 4 (Octiber 1977): 519-41.

Acknowledgments (continued from p. iv)

Document 1: From Jonathan Edwards, *A Faithful Narrative of the Surprising Work of God*, in *The Great Awakening*, ed. C. C. Goen, vol. 4 of *The Works of Jonathan Edwards* (New Haven, Conn.: Yale University Press, 1972).

Document 2: Reprinted from Douglas C. Stenerson, ed., "An Anglican Critique of the Early Phase of the Great Awakening in New England: A Letter by Timothy Cutler," *William and Mary Quarterly*, 3d ser., 30, no. 3 (July 1973): 480–87. Permission granted by the Omohundro Institute of Early American History and Culture.

Document 4: Reprinted with permission of *Anglican and Episcopal History (Historical Magazine of the Protestant Episcopal Church*, 46, no. 3 [Sept. 1977]: 303–7).

Document 6: The Historical Society of Pennsylvania (HSP).

Document 9: Reprinted from Michael Crawford, ed., "The Spiritual Travels of Nathan Cole," *William and Mary Quarterly*, 3d ser., 33, no. 1. Permission granted by the Omohundro Institute of Early American History and Culture.

Document 11: Northern Illinois University Press.

Document 12: From the Roger Family Papers, courtesy of The New-York Historical Society.

Document 13: Reprinted from Douglas L. Winiarski, ed., "Souls Filled with Ravishing Transport: Heavenly Visions and the Radical Awakening in New England," *William and Mary Quarterly*, 3d ser., 61, no. 1 (Jan. 2004). Permission granted by the Omohundro Institute of Early American History and Culture.

Document 17: Joanna Brooks and John Saillant. "Face Zion Forward." *First Writers of the Black Atlantic, 1785–1798*, pp. 49–53. © 2002 by Joanna Brooks and John Saillant. Reprinted by permission of University Press of New England, Hanover, N.H.

Document 18: From Jonathan Edwards, *The Distinguishing Marks of a Work of the Spirit of God*, in *The Great Awakening* ed. C. C. Goen, vol. 4 of *The Works of Jonathan Edwards* (New Haven, Conn.: Yale University Press, 1972).

Document 27: From *The Carolina Backcountry on the Eve of the Revolution: The Journal and Other Writings of Charles Woodmason, Anglican Itinerant*, edited by Richard J. Hooker. Copyright © 1953 by the University of North Carolina Press, renewed 1981 by Richard J. Hooker. Published for the Omohundro Institute of Early American History and Culture. Used by permission of the publisher.

Document 29: Beinecke Rare Book and Manuscript Library, Yale University.

Index

A.M., 141
   State of Religion in New England, The, 16,
     94–98
Act for Establishing Religious Freedom, 22,
   142
Adams, Eliphalet, 107, 108
adult baptism, 20, 135–36. *See also*
   baptism
Advertisement of Whitefield Engravings
   (Franklin), 55
African Americans. *See also* slaves and
   slavery
   baptism of, 119
   evangelicalism and, 19, 112–15
   leadership by, 19
   Loyalist, 86
   Northampton revival and, 36
   religious lives of, 118–19
   social status of, 12–13, 25
African religions, 19, 119
American Revolution
   chronology, 142
   Great Awakening and, vii, 22–24
Anabaptists, 40. *See also* Baptists
Anglican Church, 6, 19, 38, 44, 50. *See also*
   Church of England
   in backcountry South, 120
   disestablishment of, 139–40
   Wesley brothers and, 10–11
anti-itinerancy laws, 14, 99
antinomians, 3
antirevivalists
   beliefs of, 2
   defined, vii
   opposition to religious fervor by, 74
Appeal to the Public for Religious Liberty, An
   (Backus), 137–39, 142
Arianism, 39, 48
Arminianism, 40, 95
authority, defiance of, 23
awakenings. *See also* revival meetings
   defined, 2

Backus, Isaac, 21, 142
   Appeal to the Public for Religious Liberty,
     An, 137–39
   Conversion to Baptist Principles, 135–36
   Reasons for Separation, 133–35
baptism
   of adults, 20, 135–36
   in backcountry south, 123, 125
   candidates for, 124*n*4
   following conversion, 20
   by immersion in rivers and lakes, 124,
     125–26
   of infants, 20, 135, 136
   Schuylkill River service, 125, 126*f*
   Virginia service, 123–24
Baptismal Service in Virginia, A (Fristoe),
   123–24
Baptists, 12, 20–22, 134, 142
   disestablishment and, 22, 139–40
   open-air baptism, 21
   religious freedom and, 137
Basking Ridge, New Jersey, 49
believer's baptism, 21, 135–36
Ben David (Jesus), 39
Ben Ephraim, 39
Bible Belt, 19
Bill of Rights, 143
Blair, Samuel, 5, 141
   Short and Faithful Narrative, A, 79–83
Bonomi, Patricia, 23
book burning (Davenport), 107, 108, 109, 111
Book of Life, 72, 73
Bordley, Stephen
   On George Whitefield, 50–52
"born again," 3. *See also* conversions; new
   birth
Boston Evening-Post
   James Davenport's Book and Clothes
     Burning, 107–9
Boston Gazette
   Church Separation in Canterbury,
     Connecticut, 127